Gender Expression and Inclusivity in Early Childhood

This important and engaging guide details best practices for support-ing the exploration and expression of gender in early years contexts. It explains how to use self-reflection, community collaboration, and action plans to create supportive environments and equitable oppor-tunities for queer children and teachers in early years classrooms and schools. Featuring real-life examples from current classroom practice, the book includes diverse voices of children and adults alike, providing new ways for readers to connect to historically undervalued ideas of inclusion and expansiveness around emerging identities and personal power. Providing clear, practical recommendations in an accessible and engaging way, *Gender Expression and Inclusivity in Early Childhood* is an essential read for any teacher or school leader who wants to create kinder, more supportive, gender diverse environments for all children and educators.

Samuel Broaden (he/they) is an early childhood author, advocate, and speaker. He has worked in various roles within the early education field and now spends his time speaking and sharing his philosophy on child-hood. He currently lives in Portland, Oregon with his husband Perry and their three (very spoiled) dogs, Oliver, Baby Bear, and Moon Broaden.

T0384808

Also Available from Routledge Eye On Education

www.routledge.com/k-12

The Gender Equation in Schools:
How to Create Equity and Fairness for All Students
Jason Ablin

Universal Design for Learning in the Early Childhood
Classroom:
Teaching Children of all Languages, Cultures, and Abilities,
Birth – 8 Years
Pamela Brillante and Karen Nemeth

When Black Students Excel:
How Schools Can Engage and Empower Black Students
Joseph F. Johnson, Jr., Cynthia L. Uline, and Stanley J. Munro, Jr.

The New Leader's Guide to Early Childhood Settings:
Making an Impact in PreK-3
Elaine Mendez and Kenneth Kunz

Empowering Young Children:
How to Nourish Deep, Transformative Learning For Social
Justice
Wendy Ostroff

First Aid for Teacher Burnout:
How You Can Find Peace and Success
Jenny Grant Rankin

Global Citizenship Education for Young Children:
Practice in the Preschool Classroom
Robin Elizabeth Hancock

Gender Expression and Inclusivity in Early Childhood

A Teacher's Guide to Queering the Classroom

Samuel Broaden

Routledge
Taylor & Francis Group

NEW YORK AND LONDON

Designed cover image: © shutterstock

First published 2024
by Routledge
605 Third Avenue, New York, NY 10158

and by Routledge
4 Park Square, Milton Park, Abingdon, Oxon, OX14 4RN

Routledge is an imprint of the Taylor & Francis Group, an informa business

© 2024 Samuel Broaden

ISBN: 978-1-032-56194-3 (hbk)
ISBN: 978-1-032-55426-6 (pbk)
ISBN: 978-1-003-43435-1 (ebk)

DOI: 10.4324/9781003434351

Typeset in Palatino
by SPi Technologies India Pvt Ltd (Straive)

To Perry, for everything that is and everything that will be.

Contents

Preface

Gender. A word that many of us may have been hearing more and more in the last few years. It can be a confusing topic. And maybe one that gives us pause or creates a tense feeling within us either because we do not understand it, or because it makes us uncomfortable talking about due to our own lived experiences or bias. As confusing as it may be, it is a topic that we need to work on understanding better. Especially in our work with children. It is important that we understand what gender is, and is not, what it means in terms of early childhood, and how we can support those around us who are on a journey with their gender identity.

Not to worry, you are in the right place! We will be unpacking a lot throughout this book. Not only will you find new information on gender, gender expression, gender identity, and more; but you will also discover spaces to reflect and think deeply as well as spaces to connect with others. I am hopeful that you find something in these pages that can inspire your practice and open your mind.

I want to make it a point to speak about the very real and dangerous world that many queer people live in currently. There are many folx in our world today that cannot be their authentic selves out of fear. Fear of attack-verbal and physical-, economic ramifications, or even death. I believe that it is important now more than ever before to dive deep into this conversation. I am also hopeful that the following words in this book can be the beginning of a shift in our world. To one that is more accepting, supportive, and kind. I recognize that in many areas of this book, I am speaking from a place of privilege; I understand this fact and everything in the following pages will come from that lens.

Gender is a very personal thing for each individual person. Everyone is on their own journey and no two journeys are the same. You may find parts of this book speaking to you in ways that you did not expect. Maybe it will speak to you and make you think in ways that you have not before. Don't shy away from that feeling, push forward. Use the reflection spaces to think deeply and use the connection pieces to find encouragement and support. This book is for you. For you to learn how to better support queer and transgender children and adults; and it may end up being a manual for how to better support yourself.

I ask that you come to this text with an open mind, ready to learn more for the sake of the children. Some of the topics may cause feelings of anger, anxiety, confusion, or sadness. Remember, however, we are all here for the same purpose, we want to give children the most safe and supportive spaces that we can. Spaces where they are free to discover who they are and how they connect to the world around them. Remember that as you go through these pages. You've already done so much work to learn more and expand your knowledge, that is something to celebrate! The more we learn, the more we think, the more we reflect, the more we can support ALL children and families that we work with.

Here is what you will find as you continue in this book:

First, we will focus on the history of gender, an overview of gender-related terminology, and why gender is important for children and how we can support it in less safe areas of our world.

Then, we will focus on practical solutions, how we can support gender in our classrooms, strategies for building equity in our programs, how to have conversations on this topic, and how to create safe spaces.

Each chapter will include many spaces for reflection. I encourage you to think deeply and honestly in these spaces. This book is for you.

Reflections!

Look for this to know where the reflection pieces live!

Finally, I encourage you to use the final section of the book to create a personal action plan for your practice going forward. How will you support queer and transgender children and adults that you work with? How will you think differently going forward? There is also a section in the last chapter that contains various resources for you to explore after you have read this book as well as a list of wonderful children's books that can help support these ideas in your classroom or program.

You will also find space for community. I believe that connection and community is an integral part of our practice. The work that you do is so important but can also be very difficult. It can be stressful, thankless, and lonely. When we connect with each other, we make our field that much stronger.

I am very excited to begin this journey with you. Use this book in a way that feels authentic to you. Refer to it when need be. It's yours!

A note about pronouns: in this book, I will be using they/them pronouns as a rule. If other pronouns are used, they have been requested by the person involved. I will also be using gender neutral terms (I.e., folx) throughout this book. I understand the importance of using a person's correct pronouns and the harm that misgendering someone can cause. I used all available sources to ensure that correct pronouns and terms were used when necessary.

So, are you ready to dive in? Are you ready to take the next step in ensuring that you are creating a safe, supportive, and welcoming environment for all? Remember, this is a journey; it may be rough, it may be difficult but stick with it. Once you are finished, you will be even more equipped to create these spaces for children.

Thank you for all that you do each day for the children of our community. The work you do is valued, important, and necessary. You are seen. You are heard. You are celebrated.

Now, let's go!

KINDLY,

Samuel

Our Agreements

In a kindergarten classroom I was the teacher in (one of the most rewarding and beautiful years of my teaching career), we had something called our agreements. I did not want to have "rules" in the classroom. I wanted to create something different, something that was for all of us. So, we talked about what kind of a classroom we wanted to have and what we needed to do to make sure that happened. What came from that conversation were our three agreements: we are kind to ourselves, we are kind to others, and we are kind to the environment. The children came up with the actual agreements themselves and I put them in the specific order because I always wanted the children to know that taking care of and being kind to themselves should always come first. These agreements really helped to shape our classroom culture and community.

I would like to do the same now, with you. The topics in this book may make you uncomfortable. You may not agree with a lot of it. You may be coming into this with a plethora of preconceived ideas and viewpoints that you believe strongly in. That is ok. The purpose of this book is to help us all think a little deeper about the work that we do and work harder to create safe and supportive spaces for all children. Here are my agreements for our time together that I promise to uphold:

- ◆ We will always put children's safety and well-being first.
- ◆ We will come with an open mind, ready and willing to learn.
- ◆ We will come with kindness and show that to others.
- ◆ When we are uncomfortable, we will recognize that discomfort and work to move through it for the betterment of the children we work with.
- ◆ We will strive to do all we can to create spaces for children that are safe, supportive, caring, and loving. No matter what.

Feel free to add any agreements you feel necessary here. This book is for you. It is for me. It is for all of us.

Your Added Agreements

Thank you for coming together to build these agreements with me. Remember, we are in this together.

The Attack on Drag Queens: Children, Storytime, and Us

I wanted to take a minute before we dive into this book to discuss the very real danger facing drag queens, transgender folx, and others. Right now, there is a huge issue regarding "protecting children" from the people and who they are. Drag performers are being attacked just for leading a children's storytime at a library.

> I'm going to tell you something very fundamental: Nobody who does drag thinks about kids. We don't get in drag thinking, 'I hope the kids in the audience like it.' Do you think that going to a drag show makes you do drag?...It's funny that when it's like Tyler Perry doing Madea or like, you know, Dana Carvey doing Church Lady, anything like that, it's not drag and it's fine. There's a DJ involved, and a disco ball, and it's gay people watching. Suddenly it's, like, trauma.
> —Trixie Mattel, drag performer

Also, just recently at a drag show in Columbus, Ohio, a group of Nazi protesters showed up with really awful signage while shouting hateful and dangerous language. These are the things that are happening everyday across our country to folx who are just living their life on their terms and being exactly who they are meant to be. This has a great deal to do with what we will be discussing in this book. The idea that folx expressing themselves in a way that feels correct and validating for them could be threatening to children and their safety is a scary idea that is beginning to gain more traction, especially in less accepting areas of our country. (More on that later). It is a responsibility we hold as early educators and advocates for children to stand up for not only what is right for children, but what is right for the world they live in. As we will discuss in this book, gender expression, queerness, and being transgender is in no way an "attack" on anything and the fact that it is being portrayed that way by a large number of people in our society is further proof of the importance of this work that we do. Children should be able to see all the different types of people in our world. They should be exposed to different forms of art and love. Not only so that they can begin to understand the world around them and become accepting of those around them, but so that they can see people who look, talk, feel, and love like they do. It is a good thing for all children (and all people) to be exposed to.

We need to stand up and speak up for those who are being persecuted for just being who they truly are. It can take a lot of time and mental health work to get to a place where you feel confident and valid in who you are-especially if you are queer or questioning. We need to teach children the values of being kind, accepting, and advocacy. This is one way that we can help to create a more kind and accepting world than the world that we are living in now.

As you read through this book, you may find that you want to learn new ways that you can advocate for those who are under-represented and under attack. Feel free to check out chapter ten in this book for resources and organizations that could use your advocacy.

Let's remember the most important thing we can do in this world: be kind.

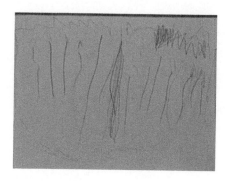

artwork by River Parsons.

1

Foundations of Gender

Gender is one of the oldest ideas in the history of our world; and is also one of the most misunderstood. For many of us growing up, we were taught that gender meant you were either a man or a woman and that was the end of it. You were one or the other. This idea, that was planted in us at an early age can have some pretty damaging effects if we feel that we do not fit into those categories. Because of these deep-rooted ideas, so many folx struggle with their identities, as to who they are, and where they belong. This idea can also have damaging effects, if someone who learned these ideas does not struggle with their identity, but are continuing to teach this idea to others. This can cause a continuation of the struggle, for folx who are curious or are questioning their gender, including children. This book aims to shift the narrative that we have been taught all these years and hopefully bring awareness to those that have not personally struggled with their identity. We will be taking a new look at gender and what it means (and what it does not mean) throughout this book. We will be unpacking the damage that these outdated and harmful ideas have caused and learning new ways to support children and those around us.

We are used to gender being talked about in binary terms, which means it has two types: Male and female. However, we now know that gender is not specific to these types, but rather that it is fluid in nature, meaning that it can fall both inside and

DOI: 10.4324/9781003434351-1

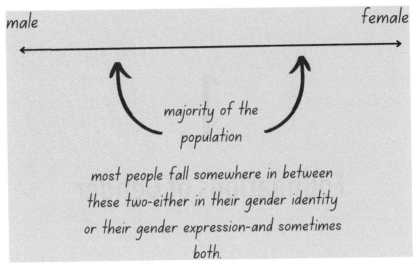

FIGURE 1.1 Graphic of a line with "male" on one side and "female" on the other showing where most folx land on the gender spectrum.

outside of this binary system. Let's begin with some important terminology that will help us understand gender better and will help support the work we do both in this book and with the children, families, and adults we work with.

Important Terminology

Gender Terminology

Sex: Generally determined at birth based on external genitalia- either male, female, or intersex.

Gender: One's innermost concept of self. Can be male, female, neither, a mixture of both, or somewhere completely outside of these guidelines

Gender Identity: How one views themselves as a person. This includes pronouns that a person uses: he/him, she/her, they/them, ze/hir, ze/zir, and others.

Gender Expression: How one expresses their gender through clothing, personal appearance, voice, etc. This can or cannot fit into the typical associations of male and female.

Gender Non-Conforming: A broad term referring to people who do not behave in a way that conforms to the traditional expectations of their gender, or whose gender expression does not fit neatly into a category.

Genderqueer: People who embrace a fluidity of gender identity and often, though not always, sexual orientation. Other terms you may hear under this umbrella are gender expansive, gender fluid, or gender creative.

Heteronormative: The assumption of heterosexuality as the given or default sexual orientation instead of one of many possibilities, and that the preferred or default relationship is between two people of "opposite" genders.

Same-Gender Loving: A term coined and used by communities of color instead of lesbian, gay or bisexual to express attraction to and love of people of the same gender.

Birth Assignment (Sex Assigned at Birth): This is generally determined by external genitalia at birth—female, male or intersex.

Cisgender: The term for a person who identifies with the gender typically associated with their sex assigned at birth.

Transgender: An umbrella term for people whose gender identity and/or expression is different from cultural expectations based on the sex they were assigned at birth. Being transgender does not imply any specific sexual orientation.

Non-binary: An adjective describing a person who does not identify exclusively as a woman or a man. They may identify as both, somewhere in between, or outside the categories of a woman and a man.

Gender Dysphoria: Clinically significant distress caused when a person's assigned birth gender is not the same as the one in which they identify. According to the American Psychiatric Association's Diagnostic and Statistical Manual of Mental Disorders (DSM), the term - which replaces Gender Identity Disorder - "is intended to better characterize the experiences of affected children, adolescents, and adults".

Sexual Orientation: An inherent or immutable enduring emotional, romantic or sexual attraction to other people.

Intersex: An umbrella term used to describe a wide range of natural bodily variations. In some cases, these traits are visible at birth, and in others, they are not apparent until puberty.

Queer: A term people often use to express fluid identities and orientations. Often used interchangeably with "LGBTQ+".

Gender Binary: The idea that there are two distinct and opposite genders—female and male. This model is limiting and doesn't account for the full spectrum of gender identities and gender expressions.

Two-Spirit: An umbrella term and identity within many first nations communities both historically and presently that describes people who live within a spectrum of genders, sexual identities, gender expressions and gender roles.

Terms taken from The Human Rights Campaign and Welcoming Schools (Definitions to help understand gender and sexual orientation 2023)

Understanding and using the correct and appropriate terminology is very important when we are talking about gender in our work. This is because it can be very harmful to use incorrect or derogatory terminology. Some of these terms may be new to you or you may have a hard time understanding what they mean. This does not mean that you do not need to understand them or how and when to use them. It is acceptable to make mistakes when you are learning; the important part is continuing to learn and do better to create the inclusive environment we are striving for. It is our job as educators to be ever learning ourselves in order to ensure that we are providing the most supportive and inclusive space for all children.

Sharing Knowledge with Children

Many people might say that children are too young to know or understand these terms. However, by sharing these terms with children and using them in everyday language and conversations, we can help not only support children who may be questioning their identity, but we can also help children who are not, by being more accepting and kind to those who are.

We don't need to have a long, serious sit-down conversation with the children to introduce these terms-they should come about in organic conversation, naturally. This can happen when we create spaces that are open, supportive, and safe.

words from Samuel!

"When I first started teaching, I was very nervous to be my authentic self around the children. I was scared that families wouldn't like it, or my administration would not go for it so I held back but I always felt that I could be doing more. Once I decided to just be myself and share myself and my life with the children, it was amazing to see the changes, not just in the classroom, but in myself as well. Once I was authentically me, it not only gave the children a chance to see other life experiences, but it also helped to create a space where they felt that they could be who they wanted to be, as well and as long as we were all being kind (one of our classroom agreements), then it was all valid and celebrated."

"My name is Shy Chanel and I'm a Transgender woman. Growing up definitely wasn't an easy journey for me. I vividly remember feeling very uneasy and confused as a child. I knew I was different but didn't quite know what it was. As I started growing up I started seeing more and more queer representation on tv, it felt freeing and

I finally felt heard by people who were a part of my community and looked like me. If I had any advice for parents raising queer children I would say to just love them for themseves, and to remember that your job as a parent is to protect and love your child know matter what."

Shy Chanel (she/her), make-up and drag artist

Another reason why we should be using terminology related to gender is because we do not want to put any labels on these words. When we discourage children from using this language because it is "not appropriate" or "bad", we are also telling them that there is something wrong with what these words mean, which can lead them to believe that anyone that identifies with these words is bad also. Think about it, if you spend your childhood hearing that something is a "bad word" or is "inappropriate", how are you going to feel when you realize that those words connect to who you are? I can tell you from experience, it does not feel good. Growing up, whenever I heard the word "gay", it was in a joking way that was used to say that someone or something was dumb or a joke. When I began to discover that I was gay, it led to me feeling very ashamed and embarrassed because all I heard about gay was that it was a joke, it was dumb, or that it was just something you did not want to be called. It took a very long time for me to unlearn that and learn to be comfortable and confident in who I was.

Gender: A History

As I stated earlier, gender is a concept that has been around for a long time. The history of gender is imperative to look at as we expand our awareness of how gender is understood across countries, continents, and even cultures.

According to "The Origin of Gender" from PBS, sex that is assigned at birth is related to the chromosomes a person is born with-XX for females or XY for males. Sex is also usually linked to biological and physical traits of the body that could include reproductive organs, genitalia, and secondary sex characteristics that appear around puberty in humans, things like body hair, breasts, etc. While these things may be used to determine a biological sex, this itself also includes a bit of fluidity in regards to folx, who are born intersex or folx with a mixture of these traits. We can think of gender as the loosely related cousin of sex. This refers to the performance of roles, identities, and ideas being either masculine, feminine, or neutral (Brown, The Origin of Gender 2018).

Interestingly enough, outside of the West, many countries and cultures recognize gender fluidity, or gender that exists outside of the binary system. The Incas worshiped a dual gendered god; in Hawaii, Kanaka malawi indigenous societies had the Maheu who could be any biological sex but expressed gender roles that were in between masculine and feminine; and the Burn Esha of Albania are a group of women who have sworn a vow of chastity and dress as men, a tradition that dates back to the 1400s.

Once colonization and various revolutions started happening, those in power began assigning certain power to a specific sex and gender as a way to create a hierarchy. Folx assigned male at birth who had male gender expression and identity were thought of as higher than those who were not. We see this all the time, even in our time. Society valued (and still does in many respects) the masculine traits and behaviors over all else. Gender also started to become linked with emerging categories such as class and race. As folx started becoming more enlightened and movements for feminism, LGBTQIA2S+ (this is an acronym for the queer community that stands for Lesbian, Gay, Bisexual, Transgender, Queer/Questioning, Intersex, Asexual, Two Spirit), and civil rights their thoughts surrounding gender and gender roles began to shift. Around the midpoint of the 20th century, the word gender and its ideals began to become more a part of broader cultural discussions as folx began to push back on the ideas of gender and gender roles.

Of course, more recently we have seen a great deal of conversation surrounding the idea of gender and what it means to us. More and more folx are starting to understand that the binary system of gender just is not accurate. However, those in power are still using this idea to separate citizens and continue the ideas of gender, power, race, and class. Which is why the work we are doing with children is so important. We are working to help shift these ideas for good. That shift will guide us to a place where everyone is celebrated for who they are. And you are a huge part of that and you have started already just by reading this book!

So basically, what we can learn from this history of what gender has meant and the way that gender roles have been assigned is this: Gender is thought of in a completely different way in many areas of the world and in many different cultures. The idea that gender is fluid and not a binary is not a new idea, just maybe a new idea to people in the west. And the idea of gender roles really has a lot to do with ideas of capitalism, racism, white supremacy, colonization, and more. When we begin to think about it in this way, it can be very eye-opening and help us as we begin our journey in discovering what gender and gender roles mean to us.

If there are pieces of this history that really sparked some interest in you, feel free to take a look at the last chapter in this book to find more resources where you can go to learn even more!

Reflections!

What are your immediate feelings about gender?

Gender in Early Childhood

When we think about the idea of gender, it can sometimes be hard to understand why this is important in our work with children. So often, adults don't see how capable children truly are. We believe that they "cannot". Right? They cannot do this, they cannot do that, they cannot understand this, they cannot understand that. Because of this, we shy away from topics out of ignorance. But children are SO capable! They are capable of so much more than adults give them credit for.

Gender is an important topic in our work because young children are discovering who they are in these early years and the spaces that we create for them can either support or harm that discovery.

"Growing up, I was so fortunate to have a community of supportive adult educators who never made me feel ashamed or less than—but, the ideas have s already found their ways into our peer cultures. Some boys like red, some boys like orange. Some, too, like pink. Some boys like trucks, and some boys like blocks. Some, too, like dolls. Even now, we know which one of each of these is most likely to give parents pause. Which preferences, especially if combined, would cause even the most open-minds to a double-take. I was the boy who liked pink and dolls and sparkly wands and princesses and wanted to try ballet. Carrying the weight of a stigmatized difference takes a heavy toll, and by the time I made it to first grade I knew that my favorite color had to be red, that I could only play with dolls at home, and that I had to find a sport to "like". My mom would tell me, on the way to school, which football team won the game—"Just in case anyone asks you." Years and years of not quite articulated difference and compartmentalization—of efforts by well-meaning adults to keep me from being seen and marked as different. It never worked—it rarely does.

The work that we do as early educators, regardless of our identities and intersectionalities, involves cultivating community for and with children. When I think about the ways that my own positionality has impacted the way I worked in early childhood spaces, the word that comes to mind immediately is "permission". I want to give children permission to be themselves in ways that, historically speaking, have been denied them. I want to work in a way where children, whatever they like, however they move through the world, feel safe, feel seen, and feel celebrated. However, I want the work I do with young children to go beyond these beautiful buzzwords. By feeling safe, I mean safe to say that their favorite color is pink or that they want to be the princess. By feeling seen I mean that I want to actively acknowledge and normalize a wide variety of preferences for playthings in our community. Different people like to play with different things, and that is just fine! Dolls, blocks, stuffed animals, trucks, all of these toys can be wonderful and, perhaps, are even better together! And, by feeling celebrated, I want children to know that their ideas and selves are not only visible, but that our community is better for their presence within it. I want children to feel how valuable they are to our community and to know that without their presence, our community would be missing something essential.

I want to be the teacher, like Mrs. Gagnet who gifted me the most beautiful sparkling pink wand for my birthday, who sees, knows, celebrates, and loves children—just as they are."

Ron Grady (he/him), childology.co, author of
"What Does Brown Mean to You?"

Another reason it is important and valuable to discuss gender and create spaces where children are encouraged to discover who they are can be found in a study from The Trevor Project that found that 45% of LGBTQIA2S+ youth seriously considered unaliving themselves, including more than half of transgender and nonbinary youth. Another survey from The Trevor Project found that at least one youth aged 10–24 attempts to unalive

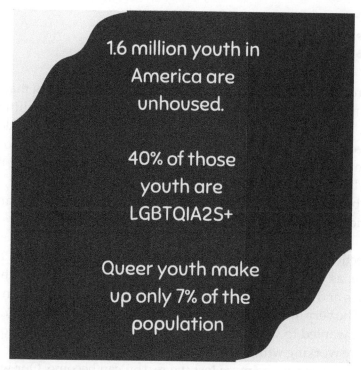

1.6 million youth in America are unhoused.

40% of those youth are LGBTQIA2S+

Queer youth make up only 7% of the population

FIGURE 1.2 Graphic depicting statistics of queer youth.
Created on Canva by author.

themselves every 45 seconds. These rates can be higher for transgender youth and queer youth of color. A key risk factor in these findings is the lack of social support and affirming spaces. (Facts about LGBTQ youth suicide 2022).

This is where we come in! These children need us. They need us to unlearn a lot of what we know and relearn how to support them. WE are creating the affirming spaces that these children need. It starts with us. And it starts right here.

Self-Reflection

One of the biggest pieces of our work is the idea of self-reflection. This is important in all aspects of our work. We must be able to reflect on:

- ◆ Our lived experience
- ◆ Our childhood

- ◆ Our actions
- ◆ Out thoughts
- ◆ Our biases

in order to truly be able to support children in the ways that we are hoping to. This act of reflecting on ourselves can be a difficult one, especially when the reflection brings up thoughts, ideas, or feelings that are not as happy as we would want them to be. No one wants to relive past traumatic experiences, or admit that maybe they did something wrong; but by doing this work, we can become adults and teachers who are more kind, more empathetic, and more open.

This book will be filled with many spaces to practice self-reflection. We will work to examine all the things above and more, as well as work on how we can move past some of those things and create a supportive and safe space for all children.

The very first thing that we need to reflect on is: <u>OUR WHY</u>. All of us wanted to work with children for a reason. However, once we are working with them, the reason can sometimes get lost. The longer we work, the more lost the reason can become. Our work is hard. And sometimes, it can be overwhelming. Dealing with all the children, plus their families and their needs, plus our administration and their desires, plus the other adults we are working with and their ideas. This can lead to burn-out and teachers leaving the field. They lost their WHY. We don't want that to happen. (And I know my reason was lost for a long time!).

This is where self-reflection comes in. When we spend that time truly remembering WHY we wanted to work with children to begin with, this can help us to reset and come to our work with a new outlook.

Here's my WHY:

I want to be the adult I needed when I was younger.
I want to create a space that I needed in childhood.
I want to create spaces for children where they can discover who they are and be confident in themselves so they can have a more positive life journey than I had.

Now, it's your turn. What is your WHY?

Now that you have reflected on and remembered your WHY, what next? Write it down again and again. Write it big and put it up where you will see it each and every day, sticky notes are great for this! Because, again, our work is hard. And stressful. And lonely. And oftentimes thankless. A reminder of what it is all for can be extremely helpful when you are feeling down. Another great way to utilize your newly rediscovered WHY is to share it with others! Creating a community of like-minded educators is an important part of our journey and one that is much needed.

Community

As we talk about the importance of community with each other, there is another very important part of this book I want you to know about: our community.

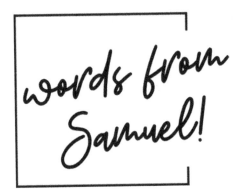

A huge part of this book is this idea of community. When I started the process of creating this book, I really wanted to create something that was different from what we usually get in an educator-resource book. I always felt like there was a piece missing from the resource books I have read; community. There was never really a place that I could go to discuss this book with other educators who were also interested in and reading it. So that is why I decided I had to have a community piece in this book. This is what the community piece will look like. If you read through this book and feel the desire to discuss it, connect with others who are reading it, or just find a space to ask more questions and learn more, come join our community on Facebook! It really is so simple. All you have to do is go to this link https://m.facebook.com/groups/265095789311243/?ref=share&mibextid=S66gvF and it will take you right to the community page! Feel free to use this community feature as you see fit. Much like this book itself, it is only going to be useful to you if you use it in the way that works best for you. So, if community isn't your thing, that's cool too!

While we have made some pretty big steps towards creating safe and affirming spaces for everyone, there is still A LOT of work to be done. This work will be hard. It may be scary. But when we take on the responsibility of caring for these young children, a part of that responsibility is being brave and advocating for what is best for children.

So, trust yourself and trust the process. At the end of this, you will not only have found new ways to support your children and those around you, but you may have also found a new way to support yourself.

2

Gender and Gender Roles

How Did They Come to Be?

As we discussed in Chapter 1, gender has had a long history that also includes intersections with race, class, sexuality, and more. We will see as we dive deeper into the history of gender and gender roles that much of these ideas are rooted in capitalism, misogyny, racism, classism, homophobia, and more.

We first must understand that sex and gender are not the same. Sex refers to what you were assigned at your birth by your doctor. Your doctor took a look at what you looked like and what genitalia you had and made a decision on which sex you were born-either male or female. Even in this assignment, there can be more than just male or female; in fact, many people may be born intersex with chromosomes and traits of both sexes.

> "Intersex: Intersex is a general term used for a variety of situations in which a person is born with reproductive or sexual anatomy that doesn't fit the boxes of "female" or "male." Being intersex is a natural occurring variation in humans. It is hard to know how many people are born intersex, but numbers are estimated to be 1–2 out of every 100 people."
>
> (Parenthood, 2021)

DOI: 10.4324/9781003434351-2

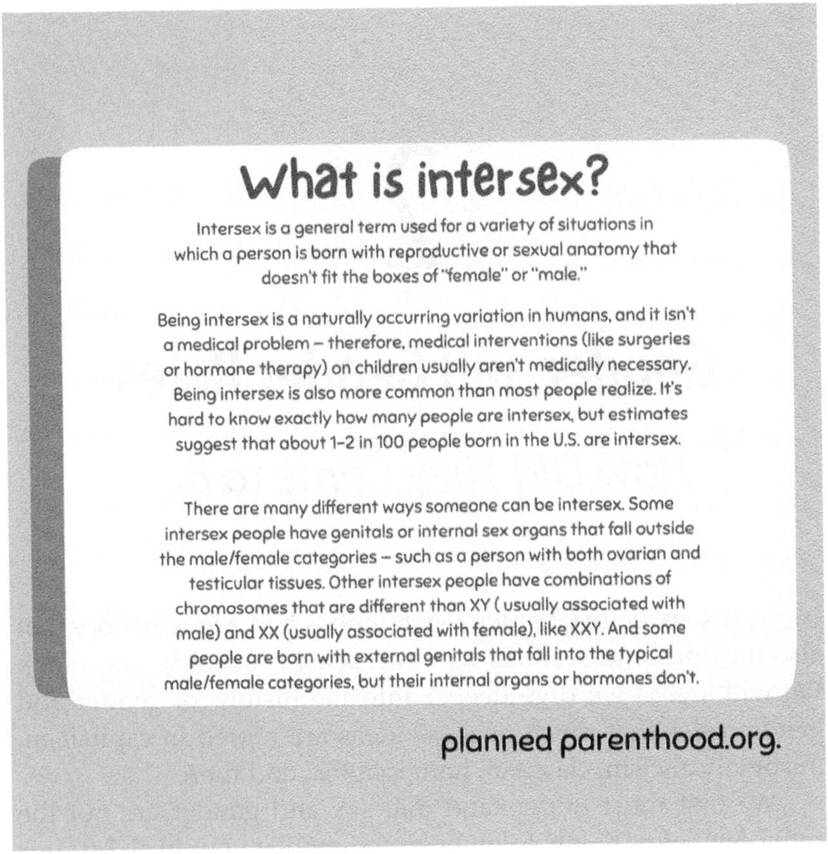

What is intersex?

Intersex is a general term used for a variety of situations in which a person is born with reproductive or sexual anatomy that doesn't fit the boxes of "female" or "male."

Being intersex is a naturally occurring variation in humans, and it isn't a medical problem – therefore, medical interventions (like surgeries or hormone therapy) on children usually aren't medically necessary. Being intersex is also more common than most people realize. It's hard to know exactly how many people are intersex, but estimates suggest that about 1–2 in 100 people born in the U.S. are intersex.

There are many different ways someone can be intersex. Some intersex people have genitals or internal sex organs that fall outside the male/female categories – such as a person with both ovarian and testicular tissues. Other intersex people have combinations of chromosomes that are different than XY (usually associated with male) and XX (usually associated with female), like XXY. And some people are born with external genitals that fall into the typical male/female categories, but their internal organs or hormones don't.

planned parenthood.org.

FIGURE 2.1 Graphic with the definition of intersex.

Created on Canva by author.

Where the confusion sets in is when we begin to equate sex with someone's gender. Gender is a spectrum with most people falling somewhere in between. Think about yourself, do you only adhere to the expected gender stereotypes and roles of your given gender? Most likely not. All of us explore our gender in one way or the other. For example, if you are a cis woman (assigned female at birth and view yourself as a woman) and enjoy watching sports-that is not "typical" for your gender, right? Or maybe you are a woman who does not enjoy painting your nails or wearing make-up, which is a societal norm for your gender. These are just two small examples of how we all may express our gender. However, so much of what we think and understand about gender has been instilled in us over generations and really does not make much sense once we dive deeper into it.

Reflections!

What do you do that is not typical for your gender?

When it comes to gender, many of us may think of male and female with more feminine traits being assigned to females and more masculine traits being assigned to males. But have we ever stopped to think about where those ideas originated from? Or even if those ideas are actually valid?

When we look throughout history and in different cultures, we can see that the ideas that most of us have about gender now have not always been that way, and in some cases, are not that way currently. Many cultures celebrate gender fluidity and even have gods they worship who are a combination of genders. Take for example, the two cultures we discussed briefly in the previous chapter: the Inca and the Kanaka malawi of Hawaii. The Inca people worshiped a god named chuqui chinchay, a dual-gendered god. Third-gender ritual attendants or shamans performed sacred rituals to honour this god.

The quariwarmi shamans wore androgynous clothing as "a visible sign of the third space that negotiated between the masculine and the feminine, the present and the past, the living and the dead." (Urquhart, 2019) Even today, in Latin America, the indigenous Zapotec culture of Oaxaca is not divided into the typical binary that we may think of, or even the typical separation of people we may think of, gay or straight, male or female. There is actually a commonly accepted third category of mixed gender called muxes-some are men who live as women and some live beyond a fixed, single gender. (Urquhart, 2019).

In Hawaii, a multi-gender tradition existed in the Kanaka malawi indigenous society. The mahu refers to biological males or females that practiced gender roles that were somewhere between, or a mix of both, masculine and feminine. These folx had very special social roles as educators and promulgators of ancient traditions and rituals. (Urquhart, 2019).

Sasha Colby is a world-famous drag queen and transgender woman who just recently won the 15th season of RuPaul's Drag Race on MTV. During her interviews on the final episode, she discussed her heritage as a Native Hawaiian and the fact that she is the first winner of the show who is also of Polynesian descent. She spoke about growing up with the ideas of the Hawaiian Mahu, a gender-fluid and third-gendered group of people in Native Hawaiian culture and society. She also spoke in detail about what it meant for her to be the winner of a show that has a huge international audience. As a queer and transgender person at a time in our world where transgender people, drag performers, and others are quite literally under attack, Sasha stated, "This goes to every trans person, past, present, and future because we are not going anywhere." It was beautiful not only to see a larger representation of transgender artists on television (the last three winners of the show before Sasha were also transgender), but to hear her speak about gender in this way and educating people on the idea that gender is not only what we in the West make it out to be; that gender has always been fluid and beyond the binary in many parts of the world and in many different cultures. The conversation around this idea is becoming more and more prevalent and it really makes me hopeful for the future.

Recently, Hawaii' representative Jill Tokuda congratulated Sasha Colby on her historic win on the floor of the House of Representatives. In her speech, she spoke about Sasha's proud heritage as a Hawaiian and a Mahu-"in ancient Hawaiian days, Mahu were considered extraordinary individuals of male and female spirit who brought their healing powers...today trans people are among the most revered members of the Hawaiian community." (Crave; see Twitter, 2023) As we can see from her words, transgender people and Mahu are celebrated in Hawaiian culture as being someone of great spiritual knowledge and very much celebrated.

When we think about Sasha's win and what that means for the LGBTQIA2S+ community, it is a refreshing thing to see and to understand that there are many children and young people out there watching who now will see someone who is like them being celebrated on such a huge platform. These are things that many children (including myself) were not able to see or experience.

There are many more cultures around the world who view gender in a much more fluid way than we tend to do in the West. In Samoa, Fa'afafine are people who self-identify as a third gender. This is a recognized gender identity since the early 20th century in Samoan society-and some say even an integral part of the traditional culture. Indonesia also recognizes a third gender, called Waria. One Indonesian ethnic group actually recognizes five genders and have five different terms to describe each. In Pakistan and Bangladesh, Hijras are recognized as a third gender by the government, being neither completely male or completely female. In Native American cultures, there are over 100 instances of diverse gender expression by tribes at the time of European contact. Native American cultures actually use a term "two-spirit" to define folx who are gay, bisexual, or gender expansive. However, this term in not the same as typical terms we use in the West as this term has little to do with whom one sleeps with, but rather is a sacred and ceremonial role that is recognized and confirmed by elders. (It is important to note that not all Native American cultures use this term and many of them use their own language to describe these folx.) And even in the heart of the

Catholic church in Naples, there is a very old idea of femminielli-those assigned male at birth that dress and behave as women. These folx are respected figures who are traditionally thought to bring good luck. (Urquhart, 2019).

We can see through these quick examples that gender fluidity, expression, and non-conformity have been a part of the humax experience since the beginning. This is important for us to understand and realize as we begin to do our own learning and research surrounding the idea of gender. So many of us in the West have been brought up with these ideas of gender for so long that we assume that is just the way it is. However, when we broaden our minds and learn more about different cultures in our world, we can see that this just is not true. So many cultures in our world have recognized that gender is fluid and able to change over time. These cultures understand gender is not as black and white as the simple binary concept we are often taught. Not only do they understand and recognize this idea, but they celebrate it?

When we think about this, it is interesting to notice that the countries and cultures that think this way are cultures that are far removed from the ideas of the Western world-capitalism, classism, and more. So much of our ideas surrounding gender and gender roles are based in the ideas of capitalism, sexism, misogyny, racism, and more. We see this in the separation of male/female jobs for instance. Men are thought to have the more labour intensive/physical jobs that pay more money. Women oftentimes lack the representation to feel comfortable or secure in those job fields and positions. They often are expected to take on the role of caregiving for children, which could potentially delay their career growth. This is a cycle that we see and understand. Wage inequality due to gender is a huge issue in our society and so much of that has to do with these dated ideas of gender. We can also see this when we look through a lens of race. Non-white women and women of color are even more so expected to work in less desirable jobs with even less pay. All of this is working towards the goals of capitalism-paying folx the least amount of money possible for a higher profit to keep cisgendered white males in power.

With the onset of colonization and European invasion, these ideas of gender and what it means really began to take shape. As we discussed in the previous chapter, these ideas can lead to a lot of confusion, hurt, abandonment, hiding of oneself, self-harm, and more.

Let's take a look at the cycle of gender roles in the West and what those lead to. When we start to take a deeper look into what gender has meant throughout time and how gender roles have been created and shifted, I think it is important to talk about how these ideas can affect children. We spoke a bit in the previous chapters about rates of youth unaliving themselves due to lack of support or encouragement in who they are, but another important piece that I think we should take a look at is the rate of parental abandonment due to a child's gender journey. Up to 1.6 million youths experience housing insecurity in the United States and around 40% of those youth are queer. (It is estimated that queer youth make up 7% of the population as a whole to put that 40% into perspective). That means that a large number of children and youths are unhoused simply due to the fact that they are queer and not accepted by their families. A huge part of our work is advocating for children. Which is why this book and this idea is so important, there are children and young people out there right now (probably in your own community) who are unhoused, feeling alone and unsupported. Other parts of this study are even more upsetting: 46% of unhoused queer youth left home due to their families' non-acceptance of their sexual orientation or gender identity, 43% were forced out by their parents, and 32% faced physical, emotional, or sexual abuse at home. Many of these parents and families may be reacting in this way due to the ideas of gender that have been passed down. They may see having a queer or transgender child as a failure, or they may be embarrassed. (Seaton, 2021). These feelings are all rooted in these negative and demeaning ideas surrounding gender. We also understand that while queer youth have a high rate of attempting self-harm, queer youth who are unhoused due to these issues with their families may have an even higher chance of causing themselves harm or of wanting to not be in this life anymore.

When we think about it in these terms, it can be very disheartening and upsetting. Our job is to protect children, support children, and advocate for them. We might not always be aware of the queer children currently in your program, if there are any. Those that are unhoused or that are dealing with issues at home could be keeping that information to themselves, in fear of conflict. The children we are caring for now could be discovering themselves and learning things about themselves that could lead their families to treat them the same way. The thing is, we never know, right? We never know what goes on when a child leaves our care. The spaces that we are creating for them in our programs could be the only safe and supportive space that they have to feel comfortable in discovering who they are; and those spaces start with US!

While this book is meant to be interactive and reflective, I thought that it was important to discuss the history behind these ideas and to take a deeper look at how the ideas of gender and gender roles that we know now came to be. If you would like to learn more about some of the cultures that were discussed briefly in this chapter, check out the resources listed in the final chapter of this book.

I want to end this chapter with this: I know that sometimes reading about history and research can be overwhelming and not very exciting. However, I feel that it is of the utmost importance that we as early educators are able to learn more about these ideas and where they came from in order to best support the children and families that we work with each day. We should be constantly striving to learn more in order to do better. When we are able to put a different lens on these ideas and are able to learn more about what gender means throughout the world, we can open our minds a bit more which will offer our children such a great opportunity to truly learn about themselves and the world around them.

3

How Adults View Gender

Now that we have discussed and learned more about how gender is viewed around the world and in different cultures, it is time to dive into how we as adults, view gender and how those views influence our work with children.

Reflections!

Before we dive in, how do you view gender right now?

DOI: 10.4324/9781003434351-3

It is interesting to think about how we truly view gender and gender roles and where those views come from. So much of what we think and believe as adults comes from the world around us, parents, family members, media, society, etc. We are made to believe in these ideas for many of the reasons that we discussed in the previous chapter; and when we really dive deep into those reasons, it can be surprising to discover what is behind them.

Adults tend to have very rigid views on gender and what it means, both in terms of what it means to them and what it looks like for the people around them. Some may view their own gender as very one-note. They see themselves in these very fixed ways, "I was born a man and I am a man so I have to act, behave, and speak in a certain way". They don't see another way to be because they have been conditioned to think in this way through societal ideas and pressure. As a result of this, they may also push these ideas onto those around them and in turn be less accepting of folx who see their gender as more fluid. We see this a lot in our world, right? We may even see this in ourselves. One of the biggest benefits of our self-reflection can be the opportunity to recognize things in ourselves that we maybe did not realize were harming us or those around us. This realization can make us feel negatively about ourselves, but it is important to remember that this is a huge step in our practice.

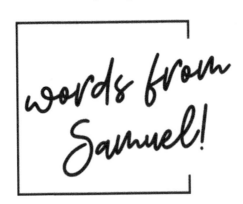

REMEMBER: We are all doing the best we can with what we know. When we know better, we can do better. We are all a work in progress.

Many adults may also feel uncomfortable with the ideas surrounding gender, gender expression, and gender fluidity. Many of us may feel uncomfortable with these ideas as well; but do we ever take the time to consider why we feel this way? What ideas are these feelings rooted in? So often, the foundation of these feelings is plain ignorance.

♦ Ignorance has a negative connotation, but it doesn't always have to. We do the best we can with the information we have at the time. When we learn new information, we shift our way of thinking and our behavior due to the newfound knowledge. Ignorance can of course be a negative thing if you are using it as an excuse to not learn more or to not try to shift your viewpoints to be more kind or inclusive with new information. However, since you are reading this book, we can assume that is not you.

This is all ok! As long as we are open and willing to learn more, and are committed to making the necessary changes to ensure that we are not only being kind, supportive, and celebratory of those around us (including children), but also of ourselves as well. So, the question we need to ask ourselves is this: are we open and willing to learn? Are we open and willing to expand our minds to new ideas? Not only is being open to expanding our minds, a positive thing for us, but it is also a wonderful opportunity for children to see that it is ok to think and behave in a different way once we learn new information. Children being able to see this and understand it, is important because they will then grow and develop into people who are constantly working to learn more and be more open and supportive of the community around them. I like to think of it like this: the experiences and things that we were exposed to as children helped shape us into the people we are today, so if we were not taught or shown that it is ok to think deeper, think more critically, and work to better understand the world around us, it may be much more difficult for us to do that now as adults; but if we show children this now, they will grow up with those experiences and it will be much easier for them to make these changes in their mindsets.

Lived Experiences

One of the first steps in thinking deeper is to recognize how our lived experiences have informed us and our mindset. Use the following prompts to dive deeper into this:

◆ Think about your childhood-what positive experiences did you have? What experiences were not as positive? Do you see those experiences informing who you are as a person today and the behaviors and experiences you have as an adult?

How did that exercise make you feel? What feelings did it elicit? Were you completely honest with yourself? Most likely, you might have felt a little uncomfortable maybe. That is more than ok; self-reflection can be uncomfortable. Sometimes when we dive deeper into our past and our lived experiences, we may find things that we had not thought about before and some of those things may not be positive. This may seem like a bad thing or come with a feeling of negativity; but this is not true. That is your mind playing tricks on you. Just because we may recognize parts of our past that are not as happy as we remember them, does not mean that we had a horrible experience or a horrible childhood. So often, one of the reasons that we may not be as open to self-reflection is because we are afraid that if we discover things about ourselves that we don't like or that we have always thought about as a positive experience but really were not, that we will now have an overall negative view of our experiences and childhood. I know that was true for me. When I began my journey of true self-reflection, a lot of the things that I was able to see and recognize did not make me happy and really made me start to doubt this "good" childhood experience that I had always thought I had. When I started to dive deeper into this reflection, however, I was able to see those experiences for what they were: just a small part of the whole of my experience and not an overarching idea of what my life has been. I hope you will feel the same, as you begin this journey of your own self-reflection. I hope that you are able to recognize your experiences for what they are and not allow those new ideas that come up, to tarnish your view of your entire life and upbringing. Again, we are all a work in progress and we need to do a better job at giving ourselves grace for that.

Voices from the Community

"Gender, in my eyes, is one of the most salient social identities one has. Perceived gender is currently one of the first things society uses to decide how to treat someone. Because of that, it is common for many people to categorize people into one of two boxes - even for people who understand that gender is a spectrum containing more than 2 "opposing" sides.

Most of my life, I grew up automatically placing people into these categories because I was under the impression that those were the only options. Once I imagined that they were not, I was able to question who benefited from this idea that two prescribed options were the only existing options - and it wasn't the people outside of these categories. The only people who benefit from the invisibility of those who are different from them are the people who hold the power in the systems that are currently in place.

In the context of early childhood education, children are placed in the vulnerable position wherein the respect they receive and power they hold is often up to the adults in their lives. If we hope to nurture kids to be empowered individuals with the freedom to be themselves, we must believe them when they tell us who they are rather than deciding to act based on how we perceive them to be. At the end of the day, we are all the experts of our own experiences."

—Cassi Cluff (she/her), 25

"Growing up I was taught that you were either a boy or a girl, and that boys and girls had specific differences.

There was never any discussion that maybe some people weren't a boy or a girl, or that people assigned a certain sex at birth were actually not…. I was lucky enough to be raised to love everyone, but there were many things we just didn't talk about. It wasn't until my oldest child was a teenager that I started to learn that there being only 2 genders was a lie. The friends my child brought home taught me so much. It is fascinating how much you can learn from children, when you allow them to have a voice. I felt guilty for not understanding more than I did and I felt awful that children were growing up in families that didn't accept them for who they are or refused to even try to understand. There is still SO much to learn, but mostly I've learned that we need to believe people when they tell us who they are and accept that humans are much more complex than sex organs. I always think of the movie Kindergarten Cop, where a child says, "boys have a penis, girls have a vagina." It's actually pretty silly to know all we know about human beings and think that gender could actually be that simple. As an early childhood educator, it is so important for me to have honest conversations with my children and encourage them to embrace every part of who they are. I want the children in my care to understand that nothing is this or that. We are individuals who do not thrive in boxes that others try to place us in. Our differences are what make us special and should be celebrated!"

—Amy Sperandeo (she/her), child care provider

Not only do our lived experiences influence our own lives, thoughts, and mindset, but they also influence our practice with children. Sometimes, children may do something or say something that triggers something in us that we may not even understand. Because of this triggering moment, we may end up lashing out or saying or doing things that we normally would not do. This could include raising our voices, using a negative tone, or even harming a child physically. Our triggers may not be our fault, they were created because of a traumatic experience that happened to us, but learning our triggers, figuring out where they came from, and finding ways to move through them without it affecting those around us, is our responsibility. This is another thing that can be easily forgotten about or not even thought about, right? We know that our work is hard. It can be stressful and hectic much of the time. We spend so much time focusing on the children: what they need, how we can support them, struggles they are having, and more. Because of this, many things do not even cross our minds. However, when we go on this journey of self-reflection, we can begin to see how our lived experiences come out in the work that we do, in the way that we behave and respond to children, and the things that we place into their minds.

Reflections!

Has a child ever triggered you?

Again, we know that the experiences that children have at this age have the potential to stay with them throughout their life and influence who they become as people as they grow and develop. We know that this is true because we just recognized it in ourselves. This is one of the best ways for us to see that this is true, by connecting it to our own lives. We also know that children are constantly watching and listening to us, even when we don't think they are. Don't believe me? Next time you see the children playing school, listen to what they are saying because most likely they are emulating you (and this can be a wakeup call for sure!). It is important for us to understand that our views about gender and how people express their gender do have the potential to inform our practice with children in a big way. For example, if we as the adult have a view of gender that is rigid and we do not believe that gender can be fluid or that people can express gender in a variety of ways, then we may bring those ideas into our practice by gendering activities in the classroom (boys can't wear dresses, etc.) or by using gendered and non-inclusive language (boys and girls, mom and dad, etc.). This is yet another reason why this work of self-reflection is so critical to our practice. So now, that we know that, let's take a deeper look at the ideas, words, and feelings that we may be transferring to children.

Reflections!

What are you putting into children?

What surprised you about this reflection? Were you able to recognize the ways that your experiences and your ideas have the potential to be placed into the children? Again, I want to remind you that whatever you are uncovering and learning about yourself does NOT make you a bad teacher or bad adult. Oftentimes, we may feel this way. We are very passionate about our work with children that sometimes if we notice things that we are doing that are not as positive as we would like them to be in our practice, we can internalize that and begin to think negatively about ourselves and our practice; but it is important that we continue to remember that the simple fact that we are open and willing to do this self-reflective work and learn more about how we can support the children in our care shows that we are doing a good job and we are meant to be where we are and that we are giving the children in our care a positive and uplifting experience.

4

How Children View Gender

Children naturally do not view gender in the same ways as adults. They just don't. They actually do not view many things in the same way as adults do. What is interesting about this is the fact that the views that children start to form about gender (and everything else in life) come from the adults around them-what they see, hear, and experience through the most important people in their lives. (YES-that means you too!). So, when we think about it, it is sort of this cycle that just continues on, right? Adults have a specific view of gender that they pass onto children who have no view of gender. Those children grow up to be adults who pass those views onto a new generation of children who have no view of gender. And so on and so on. Until someone stops the cycle and creates a new one. Guess who that someone is? Yup, you!

Some people may think that children do have a view of gender, gender roles, and what they mean because they may have seen children say things like, "you can't play with that, that's for girls!" or something similar. However, these ideas did not come naturally to children, because these ideas are not natural to begin with. Children are born without any preconceived notions or ideas about the world around them. The people around them begin to place those ideas into their heads from a very early age. So, when we hear children say things like that, they are really just repeating words and ideas that they have

DOI: 10.4324/9781003434351-4

heard. Which is why a huge piece of our work is also helping to support and teach the parents and families about these ideas, which we will get into in later chapters.

There are many ways that we can tell that children's view of gender is very different from a typical adult. Just the fact that children will play or dress in ways that are not typical of their assumed gender (we should never assume a child's gender and gender expression until explicitly told) shows us that they don't have the same concepts about gender as we do. How many adult men would you expect to see dressing up in princess clothes for fun for example compared to how many male-identifying children do the same thing. Children have a much simpler (and kinder) view of the world and those around them, than adults tend to. We see this in many other ways than just in gender or gender expression; we see this in children not caring about differences they notice in each other (skin color, disability, family structure, etc.) but rather being curious (which is natural) about differences, maybe asking about them, and then moving on with their day. Whereas with adults, we already know that many adults in our world today care a great deal about the differences they notice in others and have a difficult time moving on with their lives and just accepting diversity in our world for what it is, a diverse world.

The important thing for us to do as adults is continue to cultivate this in children. We don't want to place any ideas in the children's heads that may be unkind, not inclusive, or that have the potential to cause harm to others. Rather, we want to help children to understand and celebrate the differences in themselves and the people around them. Help them to understand the importance of those differences, how we can celebrate them, and also how we can advocate for all people. Again, this starts with us.

As a teacher, I always knew that this was the type of environment that I wanted to provide for children. Remembering my WHY, wanting to offer children something that I did not have, really helped me in figuring out how to create and cultivate this type of environment for the children. Because of this, I was able to create a community in our classroom that was based on kindness and celebration of ourselves. Knowing that it started with me was important as well, because it let me know that I had to do the work within myself first in order to help support children in this. This is the self-reflection work that we have been talking about. I have to be honest with you, it wasn't always easy. Quite the opposite actually. As we have discussed, being reflective with yourself, your lived experiences, and your views can be a surprising journey. Once I was able to go through that and better understand where I was coming from as an educator and a person, I was able to begin to create this environment for children. (revisit your WHY!)

As I was creating this environment, I was pleasantly surprised to see with my own eyes the views (or lack thereof) that children had in regards to gender. I began to notice how the children would play and explore without any ideas interrupting their play or creativity. I also saw this when I began to be authentically myself around the children. When the children learned that I was queer, when they found out I had a husband, and when they met him I was able to see that the children really did not think any differently about it than if I had told them I was straight and was married to a woman. They were curious, yes. A few of them asked "how can you have a husband?" and I would respond, "people can marry whoever they want as long as they really want to" and then they would say "oh, ok" and we would move on. See, curiosity is normal and should not be shamed. Everyone is curious, that is how things happen in our world, we are curious about something so we ask questions and we learn something new or create something new. When we answer children's curiosities with honest answers, we show them that there is nothing to be embarrassed or ashamed of in asking questions, being curious, or being yourself. Children then began to just talk about my husband as anyone else would talk about a "typical" opposite sex marriage. They would ask about him all the time, how he was, what we did the night before, etc. This really showed me that children truly do not have any preconceived ideas surrounding gender (and a lot of other things). By me being who

I am, being authentically myself, and being honest with the children, I was able to create a space that celebrated differences rather than push them away. The classroom became a beautiful place where everyone could be who they wanted to be, who they were; they could participate in things that interested them no matter who the activity was "made for". We danced and sang, climbed trees, raced, built towers and knocked them down, played rough, did art, performed skits, and listened to all kinds of music. Honestly, for me it was a very freeing experience, one that I had not had growing up. It is an interesting thing to think about, the work that we are doing on ourselves to strengthen our practice, really can help to strengthen ourselves and show us a different viewpoint than we may have had as a child. It can be healing in a way, which is a beautiful and much needed thing for many of us.

Don't take my word for it though! Take theirs:

"I just really love playing with rollie-pollies and finding them and keeping them safe."
—River Parsons (he/him), 5 when asked about what makes a person their gender

"That you don't have to do all the work, you get to play any game you want like tug-a-rope or whatever game it is, and you don't have to do a lot of work. You can help out if you want to."
—Harper Travis (she/her), 8 when asked what she likes about being a child

Harper is my husband's goddaughter and when her mother was talking to her about this question, she asked her if she remembered that "Uncle P" was married and her response without any hesitation or confusion was, "uh yeah, to Mr. Uncle P"-which would be me. Just goes to show that children view things in a much kinder and simpler way than we do as adults.

Now it is time for you to think about your classroom. How do you see children viewing gender and gender roles each day? Do you see something similar to what I have seen? Different?

Reflections!

How do the children in your life view gender and what do you see about this in your daily practice?

As you were going through that reflection exercise, did you notice things that maybe you had not noticed before? That can happen when we begin to do this work of self-reflection regarding our classrooms, there are many things that we may not notice on a daily basis, mostly because when we are around things every day, for a long period of time, we don't notice as much. It is a lot like that idea of "nose-blindness", right? I don't really notice how much my house smells like my dogs until I am away from my home for a while and return and think to myself, "wow, how did I not notice this before?". (This is not shade to my dogs at all, sorry boys!) This is a great part of self-reflection though. It really gives us a chance to see things in a new light; and when we can see things in a different way, we can respond differently and create a different space if need be.

It is also interesting to think about the reflection you just did and see what you observed that may be influenced by you. Were there any things that you noticed as you reflected that you could see came from you? For example, did you notice that not as many of the boys in your classroom were playing with the more typical girl activities? If so, why is that? Is it because you have allowed your own bias on this topic to permeate into your classroom? Are they not playing with those items because you have told them not to-either with your words or your actions? These are important things to think about because we all have done that at some point. We all have let our bias in certain areas creep into our classrooms, that does not mean that we are bad teachers, it means we are humxn! The only difference is we are beginning to do the work to notice these instances and work through them-that is something that not everyone can or is willing to do.

Another interesting thing to look at as we reflect on our reflection is how can our own perspective be shifted based on our observations? Remember when I said earlier that so much of the work that we do with and for children can also be supportive of the work we are doing on ourselves? Well, this is the same idea. Let's say that we have a fairly rigid view of gender and have brought those ideas (whether intentionally or not) into our classrooms. Once we begin to truly observe how the children truly understand and view gender, we may begin to think a bit differently about it as well. Sometimes seeing things through the lens and view of a child can have a huge impact on ourselves and our thinking. We can observe and see how children move through the world around them and we can be inspired by their much freer way of thinking to think differently about our own lives, ideas, and views. This is such a wonderful part of our work, isn't it? When we teach, we also learn.

This observation and reflection can also be a really powerful tool when it comes to discussing these ideas with the families and parents of your programs. We will talk a little more in depth about talking with families and parents about these ideas later in chapter seven, but for now it is important to note that what we discover in these observations can be great examples for the families and parents to see how their children (and others) explore these ideas. So often, families and parents might not have a fluid view of gender (or childhood in general for that matter). However, when we begin to do the work to create more supportive and safe spaces for all the children we spend time with, being able to offer examples of what we have observed and seen in our classroom as a way to help families better understand this idea can be a really helpful tool. I always say that when we are trying to get someone to think differently about a topic in early childhood, it is always a good idea to have stories and examples of how we have seen it work to help convince folx. That is why I am constantly telling stories about my practice. I feel that stories are absolutely the best way to connect with each other.

Think about the reflection you just did on your classroom; are you able to see the ways in which the children in your classroom view or think about gender? Are you able to see any influence on their ideas? Were you able to recognize things that possibly need to shift?

Reflections!

What could you shift in your practice to better support this?

5

How Children Explore Gender

One of the things that is important to understand in our practice is not only how children view and think about gender as a whole, but how they may be expressing and exploring ideas surrounding gender and who they are in the classroom each day. So often, we may read books or articles on topics that intrigue us in our work, but rarely can find tangible examples of what things may look like in our specific practice. It is also important for us to recognize ways that children may be exploring gender, themselves, and their identity, that we may not previously have thought of before. I know for me, so many things happen throughout the day and I am sure there are so many things that I may miss each day. I may not notice how the children are discovering something in a certain area of the classroom or might not notice the conversations that may be happening around a certain topic or idea. We can't see it (or hear it!) alright? So, it can be very helpful for us to take some time to really dive into these things so that we can get a better look at them and can go forward with a reminder to pay closer attention to things we may overlook each day. This is not only a good thing to do when it comes to this idea of gender, but it can also be helpful to pay more attention in general to what the children are doing, saying, learning, discovering, and playing each day. Let's face it, our days are hectic most of the time. We are trying to do a hundred things at once while ensuring that the children are safe and enjoying their time with us.

DOI: 10.4324/9781003434351-5

It can be super- overwhelming and because of this, we often may be missing out on some wonderful experiences and observations. I know it is much easier said than done, but if you can try to take some things off of your plate (c'mon now, we all know there are probably a handful of things that we worry about during the day that we actually do not need to be worrying about), and work to pay a bit more attention to the more ordinary things in your day, I promise you that you will begin to notice so much more and will begin to see a little more deeply into the minds of your children.

> ◆ A note about our programs: Before we dive any deeper into how children explore and explore gender in the areas of our classroom and how we can support that, I think it is important to begin with making sure that everyone is on the same page and everyone understands what your program and classroom stands for. It is imperative that the families, parents, other teachers, and children all understand what values your classroom holds. Letting them know how children are viewed in your program, how they are treated, and how they are allowed to express themselves and discover who they are. This can be done during an orientation before a new family joins, in the family handbook, or throughout their time with us. (Or all three!). However you do it, we want to make sure that we have done that before we move onto any shifts or changes that we are planning to make to our program. Everyone that is involved in your program or classroom needs to understand these things so they will know how to respond to others and themselves and can make a decision for themselves if that is something they are willing to do.

How Children Explore

We know that children are exploring, learning, and discovering each day throughout the day. There are so many things that are new to them and the environment that we build with them, can help support this discovery. We see this as we observe them in the environment. We hear this as we listen to the conversations that they are having with each other and themselves. We witness this each day when we see them discover something new or a new way to do something. Maybe they are learning about the movement of water in the sandbox by creating blocks or dams to stop water from flowing and direct it another way by moving the stream they made. In this example, we see them thinking, trying things out, assessing, thinking some more, and making changes. Maybe they are exploring different art mediums, seeing how oil pastels feel as opposed to crayons and deciding which one they want to use for their picture and possibly finding a new favourite way to make art. We can see this in so many things throughout our day-from the sandbox to the art area. Children are constantly trying new things and eager to learn more. It is our job as educators to encourage and support children in these discoveries by creating spaces for them to explore freely. Here are just a few ways that we can do that.

Let's talk about what I mean when I say "freely". So often, we see classrooms or programs that say they offer the children "free play" or that they are "child-led", but when we take a deeper look at these programs, this is not really true. Free play is not free if the teacher is choosing which activities the children can do. Free choice is not free if there are certain areas that are closed to the children. When I am talking about "free play" throughout this book, I mean just that. Play that is completely chosen by the children. They choose how to play, where to play, what to play, and with whom. Sometimes, this can be hard for us to put into practice. This comes from our need to control. We feel like we need to control the children in order to have a "good class". This is also something a lot of us were taught when we were going through our education to become a teacher, right? Children need to listen, they need to be respectful, they need to do what the teacher says because they don't know any better. These are all ideas that need to be reframed. The time that children spend with us should not be time that they are controlled. It should be time for them to learn and play freely. Discovering new and exciting things at their own pace. Our job as adults is to support that discovery and add to it when necessary. The children are only with us for such a short amount of time and when they leave us and go onto (most likely) a public-school environment, they will be controlled for years to come. They will have to sit a certain way, do their work in the "right" way, and do exactly what the adults tell them to do. The time they have with us may very well be the only time in their lives where they can be free to do what they want and discover the world around them as they see fit. Let's celebrate that and pour into that. So, remember, when you are talking about free play, are you really?

♦ Offering free play time: time that is truly free for the children to play as they will with the materials they choose with little or no adult interruption.

♦ Encourage deeper thinking: when children come up to us to tell us about something they did or created, instead of just saying "good job", encourage the children to think by asking them, "how did you make this?", "why did you make this?" "did anything not work for you, or was it really easy?" When we do this, not only are we encouraging the children to think deeper about their ideas but we are offering them opportunities to learn at their own pace.

♦ Create provocations based on the children's interests: instead of putting things on the shelves that we think the children should be interested in, have a conversation with them or just simply listen to them talk amongst themselves and create activities and provocations that they are interested in. If you overhear the children talking about gardening all week for example, use your adult brain to create a gardening activity or project. This way, the children not only see and understand that their thoughts and desires are valid, but they will also learn so much more because it is something they are interested in and helped create.

These are important steps to take in our classrooms in general because it will help us to create an environment where children are respected, understood, and celebrated for who they are.

If we create a culture in our classroom or program where children are encouraged to talk about what their interests are and we use those interests to create materials and provocations for them to explore with, they will begin to understand the power that they have in themselves. This will help them not only in their learning, but in their own self-discovery as well.

How Children Explore Gender

The same way that children explore art, or science, or literature, they also explore gender; what it means, what it means to them, and who they are. These may seem like very grandiose ideas that you may not think children are capable of thinking about or understanding. You're right, these are really deep and meaningful ideas. However, children ARE capable of understanding these ideas. Children ARE capable of thinking deeper about themselves and the world around them. Children ARE so much more capable than we as adults tend to give them credit for.

Reflections!

What do you think children are capable of?

So much of what children do is based on what they see, hear, and experience, right? They explore and try to make sense of the world around them; the people they interact with, the things they watch, and the words they hear others say. They are constantly trying to figure things out, find out how the world works, find out where they fit into it, figure out what they like and don't like; all of this is happening throughout the day, each and every day.

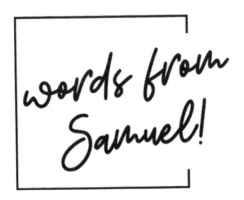

REMEMBER: Children have only been on the earth for such a short amount of time and there is so much they are trying to learn and make sense of. The world can be a very scary and over-whelming place for us as adults, so we need to remember how it must feel for children!

So, in this regard, we can agree that children are spending their days discovering and exploring new ideas and beginning to form their own viewpoints on the world around them.

Before we dive into how children explore gender in our classrooms, take a moment and think how you may see children exploring these ideas in your classroom. Think about the things you notice children saying and doing in the different interest areas of your classroom. Pay attention to the ideas you see them creating for themselves. Write down a few observations you have had in the space provided and then compare those with the ideas I lay out of how children explore gender.

Were you able to make some connections based on the observations you have done on the children in your classroom? Were there things that surprised you when you sat and took a minute to think? Or were you not able to think of anything at all? Either way, you did great!

REMEMBER: there are no right/wrong answers in these reflections, the point is for you to be honest and use your responses to guide your journey through this book.

Voices from the Field

"Experiences, good, bad, and everything in between, shape our worldview. This is true of everyone, through the lens the view is seen through is as unique as snowflakes that fall from the sky.

Our personal responsibility to others, our place in and of the world, and equality guide our moral compass and become the framework for how we show up in our everyday lives.

This is why representation matters.

That neighbour who opted out of tag football and preferred to sit cross-legged and pick dandelions near a tree just as I did. The classmate I walked home from school with who the other boys teased and called a 'sissy.' My mother's first cousin who we knew "couldn't come around," but when the coast was clear, he'd come by in his white Thunderbird to visit his favourite cousin and take us for ice cream. My father, with his soothing voice, shared all of my favourite things: an immaculate house, a love for musicals, and dolls. Before I had a name for the word, I had a feeling: Friendship, Connection, and Love.

If those people hadn't been radically themselves, showing up fully at a time when certain parts of society would rather burn than allow them in, my worldview would not be what it is today. I wouldn't understand that gender identity doesn't matter, outward expression doesn't matter, and who another loves doesn't matter. It matters that we see one another, that we build relationships with one another, and that we love one another.

I created the culture of my learning environment with this framework in mind, in hopes that children who are as different as the snowflakes that fall from the sky can land next to one another and find kinship in their shared human experience."

—Kisa Marx (she/her), child care provider

Let's spend some time diving into the typical learning areas of our classrooms and how children may explore the ideas of gender, gender roles, and how those ideas fit into their world. It is also important for us as adults to understand how we can support children in making these discoveries so I have also included a few suggestions for each learning area here as well.

Dramatic Play/Home-Living: This is probably the most obvious area in the classroom that we think about when we think of how children may explore gender, right? It is always the first one I think of because it is literally where children are acting out scenarios and relationships. Here are some ways that children may be exploring the ideas of gender and gender roles in this area:

◆ Playing dress up and dressing in clothes that may not be typical for the child's assumed gender. (Boys wearing dresses, girls wearing construction clothes, etc.)
◆ Acting out relationships. (Playing mom and dad, exploring what each of those roles are responsible for, mom cooks the dinner, dad goes to work...)
◆ Acting out jobs. (We may see children pretending to do different jobs and exploring who does those jobs. Boys have these jobs, girls have these jobs)
◆ Make believe. (Children may use this area to let their imagination run wild. This could be an area where the children feel safe to pretend to be anyone)

How you can support in this area:

◆ Encourage children to play as they will, there should be no gendered materials or ideas.
◆ Create conversation around these ideas when you see it come up. ("you can't wear that dress Joshua, it is for girls!" "well, actually clothes are for everyone so if you like it, you can wear it!"
◆ Be sure that the language you are using is not gendered and is inclusive. This may take a concerted effort, but it is important because, as we discussed previously, children are constantly watching and listening to us.

Art: This area of the classroom should be an area where children are encouraged to be creative and use art as a way to express themselves. Here are some ways that children may explore gender while doing art:

◆ Self-portraits. Children may use art materials to create pictures of themselves. They should be encouraged to use different art mediums to truly express themselves. They may create pictures of themselves that don't resemble what they look like to us, but that is ok!

◆ Creativity. Again, this area should be a space for children to be creative. And creativity has no right or wrong way to do it. Art is a way for us to express who we are and how we are thinking, it should be the same for children. We may see them creating pictures depicting gender and gender roles as they see them. We may also see them using performance art as a way to express themselves as well-singing, dancing, etc.

◆ Time alone. Sometimes, art can be very personal so the children may choose to participate in their art alone and away from others-this is ok!

How you can support in this area:

◆ Provide plenty of different art materials for the children to use. Think outside the box when you are thinking of what materials to add. (This is a great spot for those loose parts!)

◆ Avoid saying "good job!"

◆ Encourage the children to create what they want and remind them that their art is for them. It is for them to enjoy and use to express themselves.

◆ Celebrate and validate the art the children show to you!

◆ Being mindful of how this space looks and feels. Freedom to sit/stand, be at a table, standing, taking art to other areas of the room that feel comfortable for them, etc.

Library: This is another area that may seem a bit obvious when it comes to how children explore and learn, but let's talk about some ways this area can be used to help children explore gender and who they are:

◆ Diverse books. This is probably one of the easiest ways to help support children in exploring ideas. Having a variety of books that show a variety of different people, families, and perspectives can really help children to see themselves in the world around them.

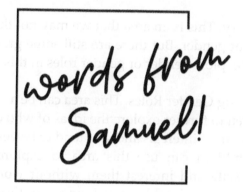

words from Samuel!

REMEMBER: it is not just enough to HAVE the books, we need to make sure that we are drawing attention to them, reading them ourselves, etc.

◆ Child-created books. Encourage the children to create books based on their ideas, words, and art. Help them to learn different ways to create books and support them in understanding that their words can be translated into a story. This can be a really great way not only to support children in learning about themselves, but it can also be a great way for them to feel a connection with their classroom and their work. Just wait until you see how proud they are when you put a book they made in the library!

How you can support in this area:

- ◆ Be sure to check and rotate out books on a regular basis. We should always be looking for diverse books that show a variety of people in positive lights. (see chapter 10 for a list of some wonderful children's books)
- ◆ Read with the children!
- ◆ Encourage and participate in conversations regarding books, children will have questions and this is a great opportunity to put more positive and kind ideas and thoughts into their heads.

Science/Sensory: This is an area that we may not think of when we think about gender. But there are still some great ways that children may explore gender or gender roles in this area:

- ◆ Exploring Gender Roles. This area can be a great way for children to further explore the ideas of who can do what. Many times, interests and jobs tend to be very gendered. But children can use this area to explore the things that excite and interest them without worrying about whether they should or not. Sometimes these things can be really simple. Let's take an example of learning about bugs. It is "typical" for children who are boys to love getting dirty and playing with bugs and children who are girls to be scared of getting dirty or touching bugs. This area is a great opportunity for us to help shift that idea, right? It is all about finding those times and spaces to create and instill new ideas into the children.

How you can support in this area:

- ◆ CONVERSATION! This is a great area to listen for and participate in these conversations, and work towards creating a new idea of gender. When children are discussing who can and cannot do something, chime in and give your thoughts. Or even just share with them a part of yourself. In my classroom, I never wanted to spread my fear of bugs to the children, but I would let them know that bugs made me uncomfortable and that I did not want to touch or play with them. Even this simple thing can help to combat the idea of "boys loving bugs and other gross things" just by me being honest. Sometimes, it really is that simple.

Construction/Blocks/Building: This is another one of those areas that we maybe don't think about too much, but so much can happen here that can support children in learning about gender and who they are:

♦ Exploring Gender Roles. Again, this area can be used a lot like the science and sensory area. Many times, we as adults see this as an area that is used mostly by the boys; because boys like to build and use blocks, right? But this can be another example of how we can shift those ideas and encourage any child to play in this area if that is what they are interested in. This way, the children that maybe would not have explored these interests otherwise (based on societal norms) now have a chance to do just that, and who knows what that could lead to. One of those girls could grow up to be an amazing architect or construction worker and may look back at their time in your classroom as the beginning of their interest and you supporting them in that can make all the difference!

How you can support in this area:

♦ Can you guess? Yup, CONVERSATION! (I told you that we would talk a lot about conversations in this book, so don't say I didn't warn you!) It all starts with us, right? So, we should be encouraging any children that want to explore and play in this area to do so. Like we discussed earlier, the ideas that children are getting about gender (and life in general) come from the people around them. It is our job to do what we can to ensure that children are getting words of kindness, support, and encouragement.

Outdoors: This is my favourite place in the classroom, hands down. I love being outside with the children and watching them explore and connect with nature. Here's how children may explore gender and who they are while outside:

♦ Nature encourages self-reflection and discovery. This is one of the main reasons that so many adults enjoy being outside. When we are outside and in nature, it brings us closer to ourselves and the world around us. When we are in nature, we are more grounded. We are more connected. A lot of times, being outside can restore things inside of us or help us discover new things about ourselves. The same goes for children. Children can use nature as a way to understand who they are and how they connect to the world around them.

How you can support in this area:

♦ Take Children Outside! Children should be outside as much as possible. No matter the weather. When we give children the opportunities to be outside and be in nature, we are giving them a connection that is so important. We are giving them a place of solitude and a place they can go to be one with themselves and the earth. And all of those things are important in a person's journey of self-discovery.

There are many more ways that children can explore gender, gender roles, and who they are in our classrooms. It is not just limited to this list. There might very well be things on this list that you can think of that I did not, that is the beauty in the community piece of this book, we can share those ideas with each other! We are all in this together; all working hard at unlearning things and relearning. Working hard to create better spaces and experiences for children.

Now that we have discussed some of the ways that children may explore gender in the different areas of our classrooms, look back at the reflection you did at the beginning of the chapter. Think about the things you wrote down and if those things were mentioned. Maybe you didn't write anything because you did not know how children could explore gender in early education. What are your thoughts now?

Reflections!

Do you have any new thoughts on how children explore gender?

The bottom line is children are spending their entire day with us learning and exploring. Not only are they learning from doing things themselves, but they are learning from us in the way that we speak, encourage, and support. It is important for us to recognize this, to recognize how we can use the areas of our classroom to help support children in learning about who they are and who others are around them, and to recognize how we can support this learning and growth in our children. Because whether or not you believe that children are capable of understanding gender, they are. And whether or not you believe that this is something that children should be encouraged to explore, they are going to explore it. The question is, will you support them in this exploration or will they need to do that on their own and form the views they will carry with them from those around them (that might not always be positive)? Every single one of us as teachers has or will work with a child who is queer. Or gender expansive. Or non-binary. Or transgender. We just will. (After all, according to a recent Gallup poll, more and more people are identifying as queer in some form.) It is our job to make sure that we are doing what we need to do to support ALL children and create spaces for them where they feel welcome, supported, and celebrated. It is also important for us to create these spaces for children who are not queer, because they will know people who are and we want so desperately for a new, different, and kinder world for all. Again, it starts with us.

6

When Children Are Gender-Expansive

When I was a child, I knew that I was different. I knew that the things that I liked, how I spoke, and how I moved through the world, was not "normal". It was a very confusing and difficult time for me. I did not have any adults around me that I could look to and think, "hey, that person is like me so it must be ok". I did not have spaces where I was allowed and encouraged to be who I was, to learn more about who I was, and celebrate that. Because of this, it took me many years (and many payments to my therapist) to truly understand who I am and be able to be secure and fulfilled in that space. This is the exact reason behind my WHY I spoke about earlier, being able to create spaces for children that I needed when I was a child; and being able to help support other teachers in creating those spaces as well. Often, people will say that they don't think children really can understand at this young age who they are; but I did. I knew something was different about me. The only reason I did not understand it completely was because I did not have any adults around me to help me understand. I was left alone to discover these things for myself. Because I was left

DOI: 10.4324/9781003434351-6

alone to do this work for myself, I went through a lot of negative times in my life while trying to understand myself. Many toxic relationships, mental-health issues, self-harm, addiction, and more. I can't help but think that if I had an adult, even just one, in my life at an early age, that was able to help support me in my journey of self-discovery, let me know that who I was, was not only ok, but that it was valid, I may not have had to go through what I went through to get to the point of being happy with myself.

When we think about it in that way, it can really open our eyes. There are children in your care RIGHT NOW who feel different than everyone else. There are children in your care RIGHT NOW who are struggling to figure out who they are and how they fit in the world around them. RIGHT NOW. Think about how you want those children to feel? Do you want them to continue to struggle? Do you want them to not have a space to work through their feelings of who they are? Do you want them to spend years of their life working to be accepting of themselves like I did? (And maybe like you did too?). Or do you want to be that adult that changes their life? Do you want to be that adult to give them that space, that support, that encouragement? Do you want them to leave you knowing that who they are is valid, important, and meant to be celebrated? Do you want them to become adults who think back on their time with you and while they might not remember your name, they remember what you gave them in their journey? Use the journaling space below to reflect a bit on your childhood and your journey. Maybe some of the things that I am speaking about also speak to you and your journey. Maybe you have never really sat down to give it much thought, but that is part of what this book is for. Remember when I said that so much of the work that we do for the children is also work for ourselves? This is exactly what I was talking about.

Reflections!

Reflect on your childhood:

It is important for us to understand how we can support children in this way when they show gender-expansive behaviors or when they tell us they are queer. (YES! Children can tell us that and it is our job to believe them!) and how we can become that adult for them who helps them to understand who they are in a safe and supportive space.

Believing Children

One of the biggest issues when it comes to this idea of gender in early childhood is that so many adults do not think that children can understand these things about themselves and when children do start talking about who they are or even showing us through their actions who they feel they are in that moment. This could be done through talking, drawings, type of play, or simple change in body language, adults do not believe them. Often the adults will say that children are "too young" to understand who they are or will just dismiss children's words as meaningless. We need to believe children. Period. When children tell us how they feel, what they like or do not like, and who they are, it is not our job to push those words aside, it is our job to listen, support, and believe. Imagine how it would make a child feel, for them to feel safe enough to talk to you and tell you who they are for you to just ignore them or invalidate their words. They may not feel safe or comfortable telling anyone (including you) anything again, and that can cause a lot of hurt. It is an honour for a child to feel safe enough with us to tell us how they feel, who they are, and what they think. We need to be better at understanding and appreciating that honour. Not only do we want children to know that who they are is valid and that we support and love them; but by believing children and supporting them, we are also showing them that there are people in the world who will celebrate them and they will grow up with that knowledge and be able to pass it on to others as well, all of this working towards our goal of creating a kinder world.

> "Be kind to your children-no matter what their interests are."
> —Perry Broaden (he/him), producer and drag artist

Before we explore how we can support children who are gender-expansive or queer, there are two very important points I would like to address: gender and sexuality are TWO different things. We need to make sure that we are not allowing one to dictate the other. For example, when it comes to a child showing gender-expansive behaviors, something as simple as the example of the boy wearing the dress, him wearing the dress could be an example of gender-expansive behavior but it could also be an example of just a child playing. Either way, it has nothing to do with his sexuality in that way. Folx who are queer span the spectrum of what queer means. Transgender people are not gay by definition. Gay people are not trans by definition. Of course, they could be but the two are not mutually exclusive. I remember so many adults in the early days of my practice telling me they did not want their son playing with dolls or dresses because if he did, he would be gay. That just simply is not true. People can be gay and be cis-gender. People can be transgender and be straight. It is important as we begin to talk more deeply about how we support children that we understand this.

Also, we need to be sure that just because we see a child who seems to be exploring their gender or gender roles does not mean that we need to automatically assume that that child is queer. None of the strategies that are laid out in this chapter involve us speaking to the children and asking them who they are. Every strategy here is meant to be used in our classrooms in general so that when children tell us who they are, they already feel safe in our space. Once a child does tell us who they are, we can of course continue the conversation with them to ensure that they know they are safe with us and in our space. But please remember, we should NEVER assume a child's gender identity or who they are. We need to always wait until the child tells us themselves.

There are many different ways that children may express gender-expansive behaviors. I want to be clear that these are not all-inclusive and also do not mean that a child is queer or gender non-conforming necessarily. It is important that we understand that it is not our place to tell a child who they are, tell a family who their child is, or assume anything about a child based on their behaviors alone. We should always wait and allow the child to tell us who they are (and believe and respect them when they do). We can, however, learn how to better support children as they discover who they are and better support them when they tell us who they are. Many of these forms of support can and should be used in our classrooms as a general rule. However, not only are most of them probably not being used regularly in our classrooms, but they can be of even added value to our children who are queer or gender non-conforming. First, let's start with some reflection. Take a few minutes to think about what support you offer to the children in your classroom overall. This does not have to do with gender specifically but more of an idea of how you support children as people.

Reflections!

How do you support children?

If you have worked with children who have told you that they were queer or transgender, how did it make you feel? If you have not worked with children who have told you that, how do you think it would make you feel? Many of us would probably say that it would make us nervous or uncomfortable. At least for me, I was nervous because I wanted to make sure that I was doing everything I could to support them. I was worried that I would do something wrong and make a horrible impact on their life and their journey. You may feel the same way, but that's ok. Remember what we talked about earlier? We are all in this together, working on unlearning and relearning to better support children, the fact that we are even reading this book and working to do the right thing is already such an important step. Hopefully, together we will be able to let go of that nervousness and move forward with new skills.

If you notice a child behaving in a way that seems like it could be gender non-conforming or if a child tells you that they are queer, transgender, or questioning, what should you do? First, you should not make assumptions. We want to make sure that we are allowing children to tell us who they are as opposed to us telling them. Then you need to make sure that you are offering an environment that is open, welcoming, and supportive so that the child knows that they are safe in this space, both physically and emotionally. This is the most important act that we can do as teachers to ensure that our children are able to spend this time discovering who they are. Again, it is important to take a look at our classroom environment and make sure that we are doing all we can to ensure that we are creating an environment that is validating to all children. Let's take a look at some of the ways that we can create this type of environment.

When we think about our classroom environment, we often think of the way that it looks first. How we arrange it, what activities there are, etc. These are very important things to consider, yes, but they are not the only pieces of our classroom that matter and that can help support this idea of an inclusive classroom. We also need to be considering other aspects of our classroom environment, both ones that we can see and ones we cannot. When we are talking about aspects of our environment that we can see, we are talking about:

◆ The layout and arrangement of the classroom.
◆ The activities and provocations that are set out for the children.
◆ The decor of the classroom.

When we are talking about the aspects of our classroom that we cannot see, we are talking about:

◆ The vibe of the classroom.
◆ The way it sounds in terms of language and tone used.
◆ The relationships between us and the children, and the children and each other.

These are all very important aspects of the classroom that we should be looking at and focusing on when we are wanting to create a classroom environment that is welcoming and supportive to all children. Let's talk about each one of these aspects a little more in detail so that we can truly take a look at our own classroom and see how it measures up and reflect to see what (if anything) needs to be changed or shifted in order to create the environment that we are hoping to have.

Layout and Arrangement

We may not automatically think the way we set up our classrooms would have any effect on how children view gender, themselves, or others, but it really can. First, think about how your classroom arrangement happens. Is it something that you do on a "teacher work day"? Do you draw out what you want your classroom to look like? Do the children have a say in the way the classroom is arranged? This is where we can begin to create the welcoming and inclusive environment that we want. Allowing children to have a say in the way their classroom is set up shows them that what they have to say, their thoughts, and who they are, matters. Again, this classroom does not belong to us so we need to stop behaving like it does. Children should have a say in their classroom and the way it looks. When children are supported in understanding their own power, the power they have in their words, in their thoughts, and in their actions, they will feel safe and more confident in discovering who they are, using that power. Think back on the reflections you did earlier about your own childhood, did you have adults in your life that showed you the power that you had? I didn't; and because of this, it took me many years and many toxic relationships with friends and partners to really understand that I do have power in my words. If I would have been told that when I was younger and showed that by being encouraged to speak up, it might not have taken so much of my adulthood to reach that place.

So, when you are thinking about your classroom arrangement, think about how much say the children have had in it, and if they did not have any, consider switching it up. Start by having a conversation with them about how the classroom feels and looks to them. Then invite them to talk about any things that they would want to change in the classroom. Use this conversation to guide you in the arrangement of your classroom. You will see the children begin to open up more and feel so much more confident and proud of their classroom.

Activities and Provocations

In the same way that we discussed the layout of our classroom, we are going to discuss how the activities and provocations can support children who are exploring their gender and can be a big part of how inclusive and welcoming our classroom is. First, just like with the classroom arrangement, it is important for us to consider how much say the children have in the activities and provocations that are set out. I know from my own experience, a lot of the time in my early years of teaching, the children had absolutely no say in what activities and provocations I set out for them (or on the arrangement of the classroom for that matter). It is important for children to have a say in this aspect of your classroom for two reasons. First, it again shows them the power they have in themselves and that the things they think, feel, and say are valid, celebrated, and respected. Second, when children are not interested in an activity, they will not be able to get anything out of it. Many times, the children may not be interested in the activity because it is something that we as the adult decided they would enjoy without even consulting them. If the children are given a say in what activities are set out in their classroom, they will most likely enjoy them more and really gain some powerful skills from them because they will be interested in them. Because they got to choose them! And now they are out on the shelves! How proud are they going to be to tell their friends and family members about that? So if you think that the children in your classroom could have more say in their activities, have a conversation with them about it. Ask them how they feel about the activities that are out right now? Do they enjoy doing them? Are they fun? Do they encourage them to expand on the ideas of the activity? Really listen to what they have to say and use that to help guide a conversation on new activities or provocations that they would like to see. Again, when we show children their power, and we allow them to participate in activities that interest them, we are helping them to feel more confident and comfortable in our space, which will help them to feel safe in being (or discovering) who they are.

Decor

It is a good idea to have our classroom feel as home-like and warm as possible. I remember when I first started as a teacher, my classroom (yes, I definitely was a "my classroom" teacher in the beginning!) was the opposite of home-like and warm. I had decided that my classroom would be jungle themed. Why my classroom needed a theme I still have no idea. I went and bought so much stuff from the "teacher corner" of the local craft store and proceeded to cover every wall of the classroom with green contact paper (!) and placed cut out monkeys all over the room. I also hung "vines" all over the ceiling, which were just bright-green tissue paper twisted into a vine. I thought it was the best classroom I had ever seen. Now looking back on that, I get very embarrassed to even talk about it but, what have we been saying through this whole book? We do the best with what we know at the time; when we learn more, we can do better. I tell that story to hopefully get a little chuckle out of you, but also to show you that we are seriously all in this together. I have been right where you are.

Some simple ways to make your classroom feel calmer, and less overstimulating (seriously green contact paper? What was I thinking?!) are by adding lamps to change the lighting, getting framed pictures from a thrift store to hang in the room, bringing in neutral coloured items like pillows, blankets, or rugs, or adding an oil diffuser to the room. Also, make sure that if you have any decor that has pictures of people on them, that you strive to show as much diversity as possible in those pictures. We want the children to see all the types of people that live and love in our world. We want to do what we can to create a feeling in our classroom of comfort, joy, and safety, much like most of us have in our own homes. Think about your own home, you probably don't have bright green walls or a ton of primary coloured, plastic items. You also probably don't have every piece of furniture in your house a different, bright color. This is because we don't want our homes to be overwhelming or overstimulating. We want them to be places of refuge from the outside world. How many of us look forward to going back home once we are out of the house? Most of us, right? Because we have created a space for ourselves that feels comfortable and safe. Now think about your classroom. Is it somewhere that you would want to go home to? Somewhere that feels comforting and warm? If not, consider what you could add or take away to help create a more home-like atmosphere. By doing this, we are creating a space where children can feel safe and cozy, where they can see people who look or act like them, and where they can come to as a place of refuge.

Let's start talking about the aspects of the classroom that we really cannot see. These are just as important as the aspects that we can see and can really influence how our classroom feels and how inclusive and welcoming it is for all children.

The Vibe of the Classroom

Yes, I said vibe. It may be a very overused word, but it is exactly what we are talking about. Think about going to a party. You walk into the party but something feels off. You can't quite put your finger on it, but it just doesn't feel right. Usually, you would decide to leave if you felt like that, right? That's a vibe. It is the energy that we feel off of the world around us. And we are very intuitive to this energy, children even more so. You know what people say, if my child or my dog doesn't like you, something is off. Think about what your classroom feels like. Does it feel like somewhere that you don't want to stay? Does it feel like somewhere the children don't want to stay? A good way to tell this is to walk outside of the classroom and clear your mind. Then open the door and walk back in. Take a second to look around and just feel. Try not to think about anything else but how you feel. Sometimes this can help us really get a sense of what the vibe is in our room. We can also ask other teachers to do this for our room as well, it can sometimes be helpful to have some-one else's point of view. When children are in a space that just feels good, they feel good. And when they feel good, they will feel more comfortable and safe and as they work through their self-discovery, having a space like this is a huge benefit. Don't be hesitant to change or adjust when the energy feels off. This change can happen for a variety of reasons like change of season or different group of children. If you are stuck and not sure what to change, having it be a class project could bring the children in as they offer suggestions or help with room arrangement.

Language and Tone

This is an important one! And one that can often be forgotten. The words that we use and the way that we use them matter. We should be using inclusive and non-gendered language. Take a day and really listen to the words you say and how you sound. Better yet, ask the children to "play school" and be you. That will no doubt be as eye-opening for you in terms of your language as it was for me! For more support on inclusive and appropri-ate language, refer to the references in the last chapter of this book. When we are using inclusive language and speaking to children with care and respect, we are showing them how much they matter and showing them that they, in fact, do deserve respect. Children who know that and feel that will have a much more positive experience as they discover themselves, and in our classrooms in general.

Relationships

This is another very important aspect of our classroom that gets forgotten as well. Everything we do in our jobs is based in relationships. Relationships with the children, each other, the families, and ourselves. Relationships are what the children are going to remember most about their time with us. They might not remember our name, but they will remember the way our relationship with them made them feel. We should be striving to create relationships with children that are strong, meaningful, real, and trusting. We create these types of relationships by being real. We share about ourselves, we talk about our emotions, and we encourage them to do the same. Building relationships like this requires time, listening, and the desire to create them. Children are not dense; they understand us and can read us as well. They know when we don't care and when we do. What are your relationships like with the children now? Are they based on this idea of control, where the children need to respect you out of fear of punishment? Or are they based in kindness and love? If you are not sure, ask the children. This may provide answers that may be hard to hear, but it is important for us to know. Ask them how you make them feel. Listen to what they say and use that to reflect. When we build positive and trusting relationships with the children, we are helping them to understand that someone is there for them and someone truly cares. This will be so meaningful to them in their time with you, especially if they are beginning to explore their own gender and identity.

By creating an environment like this, we are creating a space for children where they feel safe. Where they can freely express themselves and learn about who they are. This should be our goal in our work. Not making sure the children can write their name or do addition; but rather, do they feel safe? Do they feel comfortable and confident to be who they are? Do they know and understand the power they have in themselves? Classrooms like this offer so much to all children. They offer them a space where they can be themselves, where they can support each other, and where they can learn who they are, without fear or judgment.

During a recent episode of RuPaul's Drag Race, the contestants were tasked with making over a group of teachers. The teachers came onto the show and spoke about how important it was for them to take part in this as a way to show their students that whoever they are is ok. They spoke about how they support children in their classrooms, how they encourage children to be themselves, and how they try to show children the power they have within themselves.

Many of the contestants also spoke about teachers that they had in the past that had supported them and encouraged them to be themselves. Many of them said that these teachers were the only ones they had in their lives that supported them in this way and that they would not be where they are today had it not been for those teachers. Many of them remembered exactly who the teacher was and exactly what they did for them.

It was a great reminder of the importance of our work and how even if we are able to give that feeling to one child that we teach, we have been successful.

All of us at some point in our teaching practice, will have a child in our class who is queer, or transgender, or questioning their gender. It is important that if we have not experienced that yet, that we use the tools in this book and the support of others to begin to create these supportive and inclusive spaces for children. It is also important if we have had that experience to reflect on it and consider if we reacted in the most positive and supportive way. If we did not, how can we use what we talked about in this chapter to make some changes? Remember, we do not know what happens when a child leaves our classroom. This environment may be the only safe and supportive space they have. And that is a big deal.

7

Supporting Families

We know that it is very important for us to support the children in our classrooms, but often we may forget that a huge part of our work is also supporting the families of the children in our classrooms. This can often fall by the wayside because we are spending so much of our time focused on what the children need and how we can give them the spaces that they need. However, we must remember that the families are also in need of those spaces as well and we need to be working to ensure that our families feel welcomed, safe, and supported as well. When we think of this idea of supporting families in a general sense, it is important to remember that the majority of the parents and families that we work with do not have education or experience in child development like we do. They are doing the best they can with the knowledge that they have. Most of that knowledge comes from their lived experiences, how they were raised, how they see their friends raising their children and what they see and learn from social media, Pinterest, and more. They are looking to us as the experts in their child's development and learning, because we are the experts! They may not say that outright, but that is what many of them are looking for in their relationships with us as their child's teacher. They want us to be able to partner with them through these early years of their child's development and help them to understand what is "typical", how their child is doing, and what they should be doing at home to aid in the

DOI: 10.4324/9781003434351-7

successful development of their child. This is a huge responsibility that we need to not take lightly.

Reflections!

How do you support the families of your classroom now?

It is important not just for the families, but for the children as well that we create and build these positive and trusting relationships with the families in our programs. Here are some simple tips to beginning to build that relationship with the families of the children you care for:

◆ Create a "getting to know you" form for the families to fill out when their child starts with you.
◆ Have an orientation with the family and the child and use this time to ask questions and get to know them on a deeper level.
◆ Invite the families to come to observe or volunteer in the classroom.
◆ Create a newsletter or Facebook group for the families of the classroom to interact with you and each other.
◆ Plan outside of school activities for the families to join in, picnics, park days, etc.

♦ Share resources, articles, blogs, and books with the families to help them better understand their child's development and aspects of child development that are important to your classroom.

♦ Communicate with the families on a daily basis, through an app, email, or in-person.

It is also important for us to help educate the families on ideas such as gender in childhood. Since many of the parents and family members have never worked with children, they may not understand a lot of what we do. It is our job to help educate them not only about their child and their development, but about children in general. This becomes even more true when a program is in an area of the country or world that is not accepting of queer people or culture. (We will talk more about that in a bit).

These are just a few ways that we can build a stronger connection with the families we serve. By creating this type of trusting relationship with them, we can not only help ease any anxiety they may have about their child in the program, but we can also give them a space that is safe and supportive, just like we want to give to the children. Because adults need that too, right? Their children spend a lot of time with us (sometimes more than they spend at home), so the families deserve to feel at home and comfortable in our program.

Also, by creating these relationships with the families, we can better support them when things are not going well or when something comes up that causes anxiety for them. For instance, there may be times in our work that we need to have more serious conversations with the families about their child. Sometimes, these conversations can be difficult or make us and the families anxious. However, when we have built these strong relationships with them, these conversations can be much more positive for both parties. Think about it this way, if you do not have a positive relationship with someone (or a relationship at all), how comfortable are you going to be to have a serious conversation with them about your child? Probably not very comfortable, right? Because you don't feel like they know you or your child, or even care. But when you have a strong relationship with them, you trust them more and you are more willing to have these conversations and come to a solution collectively.

Oftentimes, parents and families may be very nervous about how their child is growing and developing. How many times have we heard, "he is so behind!", or "I am worried she is not going to learn this in time!"? They can be very worried that something is "wrong" with their child. In these situations, we as the adult and the teacher can help support the family in understanding that all children learn in their own way and at their own pace and that nothing is "wrong" with them. We can help ease their anxiety because we have built a trusting relationship with them. In this same way, we can help support parents and families of children in our program who are gender-expansive, queer, or transgender.

We know from experience that when children show behaviours that are gender-expansive or fluid, it can make adults very uncomfortable. This can be even more so the truth when it is the parent or family of the child. This is most likely because in our society, people who are queer or gender-fluid are not looked on in a positive light. Families may worry that their child will be bullied, or not accepted. They may worry about what other people may think, or they may be struggling with their own feelings with gender. Whatever it is, it is our job to help support them through this in a safe, loving, and inclusive way. Let's take a look at some ways that we can support families of the children in our program who are queer:

◆ Have an open space. We need to make sure that our classroom is an open space for conversation, feelings, thoughts, and emotions. Much like how we talked about not knowing what happens when the children go home, the space that we create could be the only space that is safe and supportive for the families as well, especially if their child is queer or expressing gender fluidity. We need to make sure that the space we offer to both the child and the family is safe and supportive. This starts with us! We need to make sure that we have done the reflective work that we need to do to ensure that we are not bringing any bias into our support and relationship with the families.

Once we have done that, we can truly offer a space for the families to get support, resources, and kindness. It is also important for all the families to know what kind of environment we have in our classrooms. They all need to know how gender is thought of in our classroom and that we support children in discovering who they are. All of these can help create this open space for children and families. A space where they can share and speak openly and know that they are not alone and that we support their child and them, through this journey of self-discovery.

◆ Offer resources. Families who are noticing their child express themselves in a gender fluid way may not know what that means or where to find information about it. They may also have feelings of embarrassment or shame that could prevent them from searching out information. This is why it is important for us to make sure that we are up to date on information and research so that we can offer these to the families. Having a community board either in our classroom or online can be super helpful. Fill this board with community organizations, groups, articles, etc. that can help support families in many areas. If you are unsure of support that is offered in your area, find a local community hub that you can reach out to that can offer assistance. Another option is having a counsellor who works with queer people come and offer assistance to you or the family. Our schools and classrooms should be spaces where families can come to find support when they need it. It is our job to make sure that we are offering that support to them.

◆ Love and celebrate their child. This is really the most important thing. Many families do not want their child to get any extra attention or special treatment. They just want their child to be somewhere that they are loved, celebrated, validated, and safe. That should be our number one goal. This is all any of us want, right? We want to know that we matter, that someone cares about us, and that we fit in the world around us. We can offer this to the children and their families and by doing this, we can help children to feel more confident in who they are and give them a much better start in their self-discovery journey.

I could sit and give you a mountain of strategies and more ways to support these families, but the best way to know how to support them is to ask them. Let's take a look at what some families of queer or transgender children say they need or needed to help support their family and their child:

> "When the triplets were only a few years old and about to have their yearly pediatrician visit, one of the pre screening questions was something along the lines of "does your child know if they are a boy or a girl?". At first it seemed like a totally normal developmental question that a medical professional would ask, but it really struck a chord with me. One, because I honestly had no clue,- I realized that we hadn't really ever discussed it with them in concrete terminology. And two, because it imposed such a limited selection of options to choose from. What if they were something else that didn't fit neatly in one of those boxes and we just didn't know it yet?
>
> I don't want their hearts and their personhoods constrained by society's prejudices, cultural expectations, or political agendas. I want them to feel safe in being EXACTLY what the universe created them to be. I want them to feel that their mom and dad honor and celebrate EXACTLY who they are.
>
> And as they get older, I also want them to understand the responsibility and importance of providing that emotional safety for others."
>
> —Brittany Deen (she/her), mother of 3

> "To be honest, I can't ever really look back at a time and think of gendering specifics in my childhood (Ii grew up helping build cars with my grandpa and wood work with the other grandpa) I am an only child and my dad was determined for me to have to rely on no one as a female. And to be able to do it all myself. So the "standards" of societal gender were not really a pressure I felt. It wasn't until I became a mother at a very young age that my views of gender changed. The pressures to be thin, be more feminine, have a man, stay at home, wear

makeup and heels, etc we're really pushed on me. It truly caused a lot of distrust in my body, hate in how I looked and insecurities that I would be alone for my life because I wasn't "womanly" enough. And because of that it drastically changed the way I showed up as a parent. I let my children explore their gender. I never assumed that they would like to "play dolls or cook or clean" because they were girls. I never told them to be one way or another. I just let my children show up and I supported them however they looked. When my oldest came forward as transgender male (afab) I just said ok. And we loved on. It wasn't a grand celebration or and exile. We simply just keep adjusting sails and loving them however they showed up because gender does not define a human being.

My children know love and not hate. They have freedom to express themselves and zero exceptions of who or what, they are "supposed" to be based on their gender or biology. My goal is to have healthy, loving children and solid humans who show up big in this world and lend a hand to others. No view of gender will change their hearts."

—Crysta Whitehurst (she/her), mother of 4

"When my youngest came out to me as non-binary at 16, my reaction was regrettably flippant and I, not knowing any better, made jokes in the house that I see now were hurtful and transphobic. I struggled with they/them pronouns. I mourned my daughter and her name. I had always thought I was liberal and open minded. This was new territory and I clearly had some biases to overcome.

I quickly stumbled upon an online group run by a trans man that (figuratively) slapped me into reality. This was my child and I needed to wise up and quickly too. Trans kids from unsupportive families die by suicide at an alarming rate.

To his credit, Elliot was always wiser than his years and tolerated my slowness and missteps. I did learn quickly, taking eventually to educating friends and family and leading by example.

Today, I'm happy to say that I am the proud parent of two young men.

Elliot is happy and comfortable, taking testosterone injections monthly and documenting his journey on social media.

Please, when your child, at any age, comes to you with a new gender, new pronouns, a new name, believe them and support them."

—Yon Flora Rowe (she/they)

Now that we have heard some of the ways that we can support these families, it is time to make an action plan for how we are going to do this going forward. I want you to think about what we have talked about in the last seven chapters and consider how you can use that information to create a safe and supportive environment for all children. How can you create an environment that is inclusive and supportive for all the children and how can you offer support and safety to the children who are gender-fluid or queer and their families?

Reflections!

Start an action plan:

8

What About Teachers?

If we are going to do all we can to create a safe and supportive environment for children and families, we must do the same for the teachers and staff that work with us (or for us) in our programs. I remember when I first started out in this field as a pre-school teacher 20 years ago. I was young, 18 years old at the time, and had just recently begun to explore my gender and sexuality. I had always been more connected to typically feminine things and now that I was an adult, I felt a bit freer to explore that. I remember two parents of two separate children that were in my class asking my director to have their children moved out of my class because they thought I would make their child gay because I behaved in some ways that may be considered more feminine or gay. (Of course, we know that we should never be assuming anyone's identity-gender or otherwise just by their looks or their behavior). I did not know what to think. This was my first classroom and I was also in the middle of an internal battle with myself about who I was. It was very hurtful and became even more hurtful when the requests of those two parents were approved and their children were removed from my classroom. It made me feel unsafe, embarrassed, ashamed, and lonely. If the program I had been working in had been more inclusive and supportive of me as a teacher and as a person, it might have been and felt different.

DOI: 10.4324/9781003434351-8

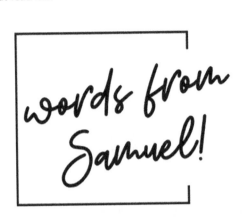

REMEMBER: we all are doing the best we can with the knowledge we have. When we learn more, we can do better. This story was not meant to cast a bad light on the program, but rather to make the point of the importance of supporting teachers.

It can be very hard to feel comfortable enough to be yourself when you are queer, both privately and publicly. Even more so when it is your place of work. Even more so when your place of work is with children. It is important for us as educators to ensure that we are creating spaces and programs that are inclusive and safe for all who attend, both staff and children.

> "We work hard to create a safe space at our school where children, families, and teachers are supported and celebrated. Giving children a safe space helps to build up their confidence for life. We make sure that our school is inclusive of everyone who comes in. We want our children and families to know that this is a safe space for them and their families and we want the children to know the importance of creating spaces that are safe, supportive, and celebratory of everyone."
> —Tia Romero (she/her), child care director

Being a queer teacher is like constantly living on the edge of what feels like two worlds. One where you are your authentic self, and you are accused of being a groomer or having an agenda, and the other where you are constantly belittled and harassed for being your authentic self, even without actually showing up as your authentic self. It's this little tight-walk performance of trying not to fall onto either side. I feel as though I have to analyze every single word that comes out of my mouth and every action I take in order to make sure I'm not going to make things worse.

"Being a queer teacher means while you may pass as straight you deal with micro aggressions like co-workers walking out of the room when you talk about your family or your spouse. Or receiving comments from bystanders about being a groomer simply because you want to provide safe spaces for young children. Or being attacked online by a local "pastor" because you provide rainbow flags as prizes in your prize box. The trauma of coming out over and over again and dealing with new families and co-workers every year means you never know what response you'll receive to comments like, "my wife and I went on a date this weekend" or "our two mom crew had a blast on vacation". At the end of the day, if my presence and being out enables students to be their authentic self it is worth the hassle and the hate. If it means that a queer student feels safe, affirmed, loved, and accepted, I will do it over and over again."
—Adriana Toon (she/her), early childhood educator

By creating spaces like this where everyone is not only welcomed, but celebrated, we are not only supporting children, families, and teachers but we are also showing children what it means to be an ally, what it means to support and advocate for those around you, and how to be a kind person in a world that so desperately needs it. We discussed earlier how children's views are shaped by those around them. When they are surrounded by inclusive and supportive spaces, they will begin to build their views on life and the people around them based on that. They will begin to understand the importance of standing up and advocating for marginalized people, they will begin to see the importance in being kind to others. They will see this, they will internalize this, and they will pass these ideas on to others that they meet in their life and that is how real change happens.

So, how can we create these types of spaces in our programs where all who enter feel welcomed and celebrated? Here are just a few ways that are simple and can be put into practice right away:

◆ Post pronouns. Pronouns are a very important part of who a person is. The idea of pronouns has been gaining more and more popularity in recent years and that is good. Asking for pronouns and sharing your own is a small step that can make a big difference. One simple way to do this is to add pronouns to your teacher bio, name tag, or photo in the lobby. This is a great sign to someone coming in that this is a safe space for them, or anyone. Some of the pronouns people may use are he/him, she/her, they/them, ze/hir, ze/zir, and more. Even if you feel like your pronouns do not matter because you have never questioned who you are, it is still an important act of solidarity and allyship to participate.

◆ Update your dress code. This is something that is so easy to update because so many of us probably don't even know what is in our dress code. However, when we take a look at it, we may find some things that are no longer appropriate or inclusive. There should be one dress code for all. There should be no separation as to what men can wear or what women can wear. The dress code should let people know that they are free to express themselves and their gender identity through their clothing in this space. This can be such a huge and meaningful practice for people. Sometimes, if we have not struggled with our identity, it may be hard to imagine how it would feel to be somewhere that you don't feel comfortable being yourself; or being somewhere that you feel like you have to hide who you are. By updating our dress codes in this way, we can eliminate that feeling for so many people.

◆ Create a family wall. Sometimes we do this in our classrooms, but it can also be really great to do a school-wide family wall where everyone can see as soon as they come into the space. Invite all the teachers to bring in photos of their families for this wall. This is a great way to show-case the diversity of your school and also celebrate all the different and wonderful types of families there are in this world. This is also a wonderful thing for some-one new to see when they come to your program for the first time. Whether that person is queer or not, it sends a message to everyone about what your school stands for. It lets everyone know that this is a safe space. This is another fairly simple thing to do but something that will have a huge impact.

◆ Be respectful. Just like we discussed in the previous chap-ter about many families not wanting their queer children to be treated differently, the same goes for the adults that we work with. If someone works with you and is queer or transgender, there is no need to make a big deal about it. No need to ask unnecessary questions or try too hard to seem "accepting". Just treat people with kindness and respect. The worst thing that you could do is create a space that looks like it is trying too hard to be welcoming, that can actually have the opposite effect and cause your space to feel alienating.

◆ Partner with local organizations committed to queer and transgender rights. This can be a great way to not only show your support and allyship to this community, but it can also be a really great way for children to experi-ence what it means to give back and help those in the community that need support. These organizations can also support you in creating even safer and more sup-portive spaces. For a list of national organizations, see the resources in Chapter 10.

Again, it is great to make a list of good strategies that we can use to create safe spaces, but sometimes it can be more helpful to hear from members of the community about what is really needed. Let's take a look at what some queer educators have to say about how programs can create spaces where they feel safe and welcomed.

"Being a Black Queer early childhood educator in a predominantly Black school puts me in a unique position. My being Black allows my young Black students to have their culture reflected to them. While my being Queer allows them to learn more about diverse people they may come across in life or may become."
—Teacher Drew (he/they), early childhood educator

"I never really put much thought into being a queer educator; I was born and raised in the Bay Area of California, there was so much inclusivity and other queer educators, families, and directors that I always felt safe. It wasn't until I moved to the south that I felt scared to share with a child when asked if I have a boyfriend, that I actually have a wife. I encountered many people who were trying to silence me when I was trying to be my true self. Being a queer teacher is still in fact a huge issue and I feel privileged to have not experienced it until my mid-twenties. But the child who is growing up in places where it isn't accepted needs to have other queer teachers in their life to make them feel safe, seen, heard, and validated. In order to see change, politicians and educational board directors need to value children's lives more than they value a book written 3500 years ago."
—Katie Heiser (she/her), early childhood educator

"In 2005 when I began teaching pre-school, I had also just come out to my loved ones and had my first ever girlfriend. I spent a lot of years hiding who I was from families but it hurt my relationships with them. They could tell there was a part of my life that I wasn't sharing and it made them hesitant to create a deeper relationship with me. As the years went on, I eventually had my own child with my now ex-wife and I really had no choice but to share what my family looked like. Being a queer pre-school teacher means that not only am I exploring and learning more about the world around me alongside the children but I am also exploring and learning what it means to be authentically me. I strive to create a safe space for all of the children in my care and in turn, I created that same safe space for myself".

—Jessica Cordova (she/her), early childhood educator

Think about your program now. Do you feel that it does a good job of being welcoming and inclusive to teachers? Are there things that could be shifted or changed to make it more inclusive? What can you do going forward to do your part in making it more inclusive?

Reflections!

9

Supporting Folx in Less Accepting Areas

There is something that we cannot brush over as we discuss gender and childhood. The fact that in many areas of our country and our world today, being queer is dangerous. We see this constantly in the attacks on drag performers, queer artists, queer people, and others. Many areas of our society are simply not as safe or accepting of queer people. However, these folx still exist inside these spaces. In order for us to fully be able to support children and teachers who are queer, we need to understand how we can be advocates for those who are not as safe as we may be.

Reverend Dawn Bennett is Nashville's first queer, female Evangelical Lutheran pastor. She speaks about what it is like being queer in the South during these times in an article published by NBC News. "Quite frankly, people's lives are at stake. It is very difficult being here right now." (Eugenios, 2021). This is an overarching feeling for many queer people living in states that are quickly stripping away the rights of queer and transgender people. When we think about what this means not only for those adults living through this, but for the children who are queer and growing up surrounded by this type of hate and discrimination, it can give us a new insight that we may not

DOI: 10.4324/9781003434351-9

have had before if we are living and working in an area of the world that is more accepting of queerness. I often think about that myself living in the Pacific Northwest where we have a pretty accepting community and are not in any fear due to being ourselves. Sometimes when we are in our own little "bubble", it can be hard to think that there are places or people who do not have the same experience as we do. Which is why it is important for us to really take a deep look at these issues and how we can support people living in these areas, both adults and children.

Reflections!

What is it like where you live currently?

We already know from some of the statistics that we saw in earlier chapters that children and young people who identify as queer have a higher rate of being unhoused, mentally ill, and suicidal. We also know that much of that has to do with the fact that these children and young people do not have the support of their family or their community in the self-discovery journey. Now if we know those things, think about what it must be like to live in a place where the majority of people feel that you do not deserve any support or any rights. We can easily assume that the children and young people who are queer there have the same or higher rates of these things. In fact, according to The Trevor Project, "the largest proportion of LGBT individuals, 35%, live in the South." They also state that "69% of 18–24 year olds [who are LGBT] had fair or poor mental health." Furthermore, this study that took place in 2020 states that queer youth in the south had 9% greater odds of past-year suicide than other regions of the country. (LGBTQ youth in the South 2022) Many of these young people reported not having access to safe and supportive spaces. This is exactly what we are talking about and trying to accomplish. These studies show us the reason behind what we are trying to do. No child should go through life feeling like who they are is wrong or not feeling like they have spaces where they can be accepted and celebrated for being who they are. No child should feel like they have no other choice but to harm themselves or remove themselves from this world altogether. Hearing this, hurts my heart and my soul, as I am sure it does yours as well. This is the opposite of what we set out to do when we started in this field. We want to support children, celebrate children, and give them spaces where they feel safe.

While we may not be able to go to these other places to offer on the ground support (if you can, you should!), there are still some really great ways that we can show our support and advocate for these folx:

◆ Involve the children in your class. One of the most important things that we can teach our children is our collective responsibility to help and support others who need it. Spend time talking with your children about how people in these areas are having rights taken away from them and how that can affect their lives. We should not be afraid or shy away from speaking about these topics with children; it is important for them to know and understand so that they can begin to learn how they can help create a better world. Talk with them about ways that they can think of to help. Bring your own ideas as well but be sure to listen to what the children are saying and suggesting and do those things as well. Including the children in this will give them both a sense of pride for helping and a sense of advocacy.

♦ Find organizations that you can support that help support those folx in these areas. We can't always help or support on the ground, right? But we can always reach out and find ways to help through different community organizations and hubs. Just doing a simple search for these organizations can be helpful, but I have taken the liberty of compiling a list in the next chapter for you.

♦ Involve the families and your program as a whole. Share with others your desire to help folx in these areas and support them in fighting for their basic rights. You can enlist the help and support of families from your program as well as the other adults that you work with. Some families or teachers might have connections that can be used to further your support. Also, by connecting with each other in this way, you are also strengthening the community around you and the children you serve which will only further push us towards our goal of creating safe and supportive spaces for all.

♦ Call government officials from these states and voice your thoughts. Government officials work for YOU. So, if you are unhappy with things that they are doing, you have the right to speak up. Encourage others to do the same. If speaking on the phone makes you uncomfortable, you can also find their addresses and send letters. Better yet, send a bunch of letters from you, the children, and the families.

♦ Find marches, protests and sit-ins in your area. Many times, folx will do these even if they do not live in the affected area to show solidarity and allyship with those affected. This can be a great opportunity not only for you, but for the children as well.

REMEMBER: children are capable of hearing, learning, and understanding these topics. We should not be shying away from discussing these topics with children, it is important for them to understand and for us to show them what it truly means to be an advocate andan ally.

One thing I want to mention, whatever you do to show your support is valid, important, and needed! I don't want you feeling like you are not doing enough or you can't do enough. Remember what we talked about earlier? We all do the best we can with what we have and where we are. All forms of support, encouragement, and allyship are valid and equally important.

10

Reflections, Resources, and Going Forward

Oftentimes, when I finish a book, I am left with this feeling of, "what now?". I may have learned a lot or may be fired up to do something with the information that I learned, but I feel stuck. I don't know if you ever have felt that way, but either way, this chapter is the solution to that feeling!

We spent a lot of time over the course of this book speaking about self-reflection and participating in reflection activities, hey, I warned you! Now I want us to take all those self-reflection pieces and create an action plan for what we are going to do going forward in our practice, to provide children with the safe and supportive spaces we know they need. This action plan should be specific with tangible steps you can take tomorrow in your program.

Think about

♦ What were your thoughts on gender and childhood before you opened this book?

♦ How have your thoughts changed, shifted, or deepened?

♦ How will you be able to use new terminology to create more inclusive language in your classroom?

♦ What did you learn from the history of gender and how can you use that in your practice?

DOI: 10.4324/9781003434351-10

- What were your views on gender roles prior to this book? Have those views changed at all?
- Did you recognize yourself when we discussed how adults view gender? Did you recognize others in your life?
- Has your view on how children view gender changed? Are you able to see more through your own observations on the children in your classroom view gender?
- What stuck out to you the most when we discussed how children may explore gender and gender roles in the classroom? Were you able to find new tips or strategies to help support that exploration?
- Are there areas of your classroom that you did not consider could be used for children to explore the ideas of gender and gender roles? How can you utilize those areas in a different way going forward?
- Have you had experience with children who were queer or gender-expansive prior? Are you more prepared to support these children now? How?
- How did the stories from queer children and educators affect your views and how can you use those stories to inform your practice going forward?
- Do you feel that you are better able to support the families of your program now? How so?
- How does your program support queer adults now? Are there things that you can change or implement with the information you learned?
- Do you let people know your pronouns when you meet them? Will that change and why?
- How did it feel to read the statistics of children and youth in our country? How do you feel about being an ally and advocating for folx in less accepting areas? Are there things you are going to do going forward to help support those in need?
- What were the biggest aha moments for you? How are you going to use those moments to inform your practice going forward?

Using all of these reflections, come up with an action plan for your practice going forward. Something to remember as you create this action plan, make sure that it is doable. Do not give yourself a bunch of goals or actions that you do not truly think you can put into practice. Not only will that not be helpful, but it has the potential to derail you from this work because when we set goals that we do not reach, we tend to get down on ourselves and give up. (Which is another thought process that needs to be shifted, but we can save that for another book!) Think honestly about the previous questions and what you want to do going forward. Think about your WHY. Think about what it is that you want the children to feel when they are with you. How do you want them to move on from your classroom? What kind of people do you want them to be? Use ALL of these things to inform your action plan.

Reflections!

Create your action plan!

Once your action plan is created, make copies of it. Put it up where you can see it. Add it to your lesson plan book. Share it with others to help inspire not only them, but yourself as well. And share it with me!

Speaking of that, let's talk a little bit more about the community piece of this book. I have created an online cohort to accompany this book. The reason for this is so that we all can have a place to come and share thoughts, ideas, suggestions, questions, and wonderings that came from our reading of this book. We know that our work is hard, and working to create inclusive spaces for children at the same time can make it even harder. We need community. We need connection. It is an integral part of the humxn experience and it is a very important part of the work that we do. You can find the community at (https://m.facebook.com/groups/265095789311243/?ref= share&mibextid=S66gvF). Use this cohort in the same way you use this book, however you see fit! It is made for you. Use it as often or as sparsely as you see fit for yourself and your practice. My hope is that you are able to find a deeper sense of community within our field and find other like-minded folx who can help to encourage, grow, and strengthen your practice as you do the same for them. I will also be engaging in this cohort and am hopeful of finding the same things for myself. Use this space also to share your various reflections, and action plans to collaborate and bounce ideas off each other with the goal of creating safe and supportive spaces for the children we all serve.

Throughout this book, we have talked about different resources, books, and support that we can use to even further our knowledge and ability to support these children and their families. I have compiled a list of resources here for you to use to further your understanding and practice. This list is in no way meant to be an exhaustive list of all the resources out there, so feel free to add any resources you know of in the community to share with other readers.

Resources

- ◆ TheTrevorproject.org
- ◆ GLAAD.org
- ◆ Hrc.org
- ◆ Welcomingschools.org

- Plannedparenthood.org
- Southernequality.org
- Find your local representatives: house.gov

Children's Books

What Does Brown Mean to You? by Ron Grady

Being You by Megan Madison, Jessica Rali, and Anne/Andy Passchier

Whoever You Are by Josephine Wai Lin and Sandy Lopez

Jacob's New Dress by Sarah and Ian Hoffman

Love Makes a Family by Sophie Beer

It Feels Good to Be Yourself: A Book About Gender Identity by Theresa Thorn and Noah Grigni

The Hips on the Drag Queen Go Swish, Swish, Swish by Lil Miss Hot Mess and Olga de Dios Ruiz

Eugene the Unicorn by T. Wheeler

Kind Like Marsha: Learning from LGBTQ+ Leaders by Sarah Prager and Cheryl Thuesday

Julian is a Mermaid by Jessica Love

Pink is for Boys by Robb Peralman and Eda Kaban

Sparkle Boy by Leslea Newman

I Can Do Hard Things: Mindfulness Affirmations for Kids by Gabi Garcia and Charity Russell

My Shadow is Purple by Scott Stuart

The Boy with Big Big Feelings by Britney Winn Lee and Jacob Souva

Bodies are Cool by Tyler Feder

The Not-So-Friendly Friend: How to Set Boundaries for Healthy Friendships by Christina Furnival and Katie Dwyer

I Love You When You're Angry by Erin Winters and Kaitlin Bucher

Pink is for Everybody by Ella Russell and Udayna Lugo

Dress Like a Girl by Patricia Toht and Lorian Tu-Dean

The Dirt Girl by Jodi Dee

Busy Betty by Reese Witherspoon

The Bad Seed by Jory John

As you move on in your practice, I want to leave you with one last thought…

YOU matter. YOU are special. YOU are valid. Just the way you are. The work you are doing for children is important. It may be difficult at times, it may make you want to quit; but you ARE changing lives. You are making a difference in the world. If no one has told you, I am here to tell you:

I see you.
I am proud of you.
I am here for you.

In kindness always, we go forward.

Epilogue/Acknowledgements

I truly hope that you gained something from this journey with me. I hope that you were able to think deeper about yourself and your practice. I hope that you feel more confident and prepared to go forward and create inclusive and safe spaces for the children you serve. Please reach out to me and let's connect more on this idea. I love talking about all things childhood and I love gaining new connections and relationships with others who view childhood in this way as well. Thank you for joining me on this journey, I am so honoured to have shared this space with you.

I have so many people to say thank you to for supporting me in this journey. I have wanted to write a book for a very long time, but never thought that it would be possible. Gender expression and diversity in early childhood is something that is so close to my heart and something that I feel is so important for more educators to explore and understand more. I am so happy to see this book come to life and I cannot wait to hear what you think!

I first need to thank my editor Alexis and the entire team at Routledge. From the moment I met Alexis, her enthusiasm for this project was palpable and I could not wait to work with her. Her and the entire team at Routledge has made this journey such a wonderful experience for me and I could not be more grateful.

To my friends who not only supported my dreams, but also spent so much of their own time reading and rereading my work, giving me suggestions, and pushing me when I felt like giving up:

Kylie, I don't know what I would do without you. Your constant support and encouragement is unmatched and I am so thankful that our paths crossed, can you believe we did it?

Megan, Emily, Tonya, Estera, Nancy, Kim, Laura and all of #TeamOregon, I love you all so much and am so grateful for our friendship and how we have become so close. My girls!

Ra-Sha-homie, look at this! I did it! I don't know what I would have done without you in my life all these years. I cherish our friendship and am so grateful for all you have done and continue to do for me.

Tia, my ride or die. We have long since moved beyond friends to becoming a true family. I love you so much and cannot wait to celebrate this with you!

To all the folx who sent in their quotes, stories, and experiences for this book: Crysta, Alyssa, Vanity, Kisa, Amy, Cassi, Katie, "Jessica" Drew, Adriana, Shy, Tia - I appreciate you all sharing your stories. Lives will be changed because of it.

To my very special girl, Harper. I love you and I am so glad to have you in my life and in this book.

Special thanks to my friend River, who provided not only some wonderful words but also a wonderful piece of art for this book. Thanks River and I promise we will search for rollie-pollies!

To my girl, my sis Ron Grady, girl, I love you so much! Who would have thought that me chasing you down at a conference to meet you would have led us to where we are now! I am so thankful for you, our friendship, and where we are. Let's continue to conquer the world!

To my early childhood bestie, Kristen Peterson, what is our life?! I cannot express how grateful I am for you and all you have brought to my life. That tour is inching closer and closer!

To my queen, my mom Jennifer. I would not be the person I am today without you. I love you so much and this is for you!

To my boys-Oliver, Baby Bear, and Moon, daddy loves you!

To my world, my best friend, my business partner, my husband Perry. I love you more than words can express. I am so grateful to have found you and to be going on this journey of life with you by my side. There is no other way that I would have it. What team do we play for?!

References

Brown, K. (2018). The origin of gender. YouTube. PBS Origins. Retrieved April 26, 2023, from https://www.youtube.com/watch?v=5e12ZojkYrU

Definitions to help understand gender and sexual orientation. Welcoming Schools. (2023). Retrieved April 29, 2023, from https://welcomingschools.org/resources/definitions-gender-sexual-orientation

Eugenios, J. (2021, June 1). Nashville's 1st Queer female Lutheran pastor tells LGBTQ faithful, 'god has not let go of you'. *NBCNews.com*. Retrieved April 28, 2023, from https://www.nbcnews.com/feature/nbc-out/nashville-s-1st-queer-female-lutheran-pastor-tells-lgbtq-faithful-n1268943

Facts about LGBTQ youth suicide. *The Trevor Project*. (2022, October 25). Retrieved April 26, 2023, from https://www.thetrevorproject.org/resources/article/facts-about-lgbtq-youth-suicide/

LGBTQ youth in the South. The Trevor Project. (2022, February 14). Retrieved April 28, 2023, from https://www.thetrevorproject.org/research-briefs/lgbtq-youth-in-the-south-dec-2021/

Parenthood, P. (2021). What is intersex?: Definition of Intersexual. *Planned Parenthood*. Retrieved April 26, 2023, from https://www.plannedparenthood.org/learn/gender-identity/sex-gender-identity/whats-intersex

Seaton, J. (2021, October 24). Perspective|homeless rates for LGBT teens are alarming, but parents can make a difference. *The Washington Post*. Retrieved April 26, 2023, from https://www.washingtonpost.com/news/parenting/wp/2017/03/29/homeless-rates-for-lgbt-teens-are-alarming-heres-how-parents-can-change-that/

Twitter. (2023). Twitter. Retrieved April 28, 2023, from https://twitter.com/popcrave/status/1651662182583779328?s=42&t=hM989RhTUZzXWQIq6Tv6EA

Urquhart, I. (2019, October 14). Exploring the history of gender exp-
    ression. Retrieved April 26, 2023, from https://link.ucop.edu/
    2019/10/14/exploring-the-history-of-gender-expression/

For Product Safety Concerns and Information please contact our EU
representative GPSR@taylorandfrancis.com Taylor & Francis Verlag GmbH,
Kaufingerstraße 24, 80331 München, Germany

Printed and bound by CPI Group (UK) Ltd, Croydon, CR0 4YY
08/06/2025
01897003-0009